Android Programming In a Day!

By Sam Key

The Power Guide for Beginners In Android App Programming

Android Programming In a Day!

Copyright 2015 by Sam Key - All rights reserved.

Table of Contents

Introduction

I want to thank you and congratulate you for purchasing the book, "Android Programming In a Day!".

This book contains proven steps and strategies on how to get started with Android app development.

This book will focus on preparing you with the fun and tiring world of Android app development. Take note that this book will teach you basic Android app programming and designing. Android development is a huge subject to tackle, and learning everything about it in just one slim book is nigh on impossible. Nevertheless, using this book as a foundation of your journey in Android app development is crucial.

On the other hand, this book will mostly revolve around the familiarization of the Java programming, XML writing, Android operating system, Android SDK, Eclipse IDE, and Android Studio.

Why not focus on programming immediately? Unfortunately, the biggest reason many aspiring Android developers stop on learning this craft is due to the lack of wisdom on the tools and skills they need to make Android app development easier.

Sure, you can also make apps using other languages like Python and other IDEs on the market. However, you can expect that using those is much more difficult than learning what Google has recommended. As of now, Google recommends using the newest Android Studio and Android SDK to develop Android apps. Back then, Google and most Android app developers recommend using Eclipse and ADTs (Android Development Tools.

On a different note, you can use some online tools to develop your Android app for you. But where's the fun in that? You will not learn if you use such tools. Although it does not mean that you should completely stay away from that option.

Anyway, the book will be split into two parts. The first part will prepare you and tell you the things you need before you develop apps and familiarize you with the skills and tools you need to develop Android apps. The second part will teach you in-depth knowledge about the Android operating system and Android apps.

Also, this book will be sprinkled with tidbits about the basic concepts of Android app development, as well as various aspects – from the program structure to navigation. As you read along, you will have a concrete idea on what to do next.

Thanks again for purchasing this book. I hope you enjoy it!

Part I: Preparations for Android App Development

Chapter 1: Introduction to Android

As you might already know, Android is an operating system for mobile devices such as smartphones and tablets. This operating system is based on Linux, which in turn is based on UNIX. It shares minor similarities to Apple's iOS because iOS is another UNIX-inspired operating system.

Here's some quick facts about Android:

- Have you ever wondered where the term *Android* came from? Well, Android is actually Andy Rubins. His coworkers at Apple started calling him that because of his deep interest for robots. Eventually, he adopted the name for his mobile operating system company, Android Inc.

- Before Google took over, the digital camera segment was the first target market of Android Inc. They wanted to create a platform for smart cameras back in 2003. However, while doing a market study, Rubin found that the digital camera market was flat, averaging up to only thirty million units annually. Thus, the idea for an open source mobile phone OS emerged as the next best bet.

- HTC Dream is the first ever android phone released to the public. It was launched to compete with the more popular iPhone back in 2008.

- To facilitate ease of development, Google chose to work with an open platform, and initiated the formation of the Open Handset Alliance. This means that users can see firsthand what goes on at the different stages of the design and development of the products. More importantly, it encouraged end-user participation in app development.

- There are more than twelve million lines of code behind the Android OS.

- Desserts rule when it comes to naming Android's OS. Starting with Android 1.5 dubbed Cupcake, Google adopted various names of sweet treats in alphabetical order to name succeeding Android versions. The latest version, the Android 5.0 has the codemane Lollipop. You can catch a glimpse of these Android desserts on Google's lawn in California.

Mobile device application development has become easier with Android. Before, smartphone application development was difficult since most phones only used their respective firmware to operate. On the other hand, some ran on different types of operating systems.

With Android, developers can just create software for it and expect that their creations will run on all devices that use this operating system. By the way, the Open Handset Alliance created Android. The Open Handset Alliance is composed of Google and a handful of other companies.

If you want to go in depth with Android, you can check its source code. Fiddling with Android's source code is okay, since it is free and open source. Android is under Apache License and GNU general Public License.

History of Android

With over 1.5 million devices activated each day, it is hard to imagine that Android had its share of blurry beginnings. Android started with nothing to its name except the team's tremendous ingenuity and foresight. It was never heard of when it started out and until the release of Android 4.0, you won't be able to find screenshots of the earliest versions of the Android. In fact, this lack of coverage on the end-user side is a clear indication that Android was almost at the verge of extinction.

As the first ever, cloud-based operating system, a large chunk of their products rely on the servers of Google to function. However, because of the dwindling number of users, particularly that of the older versions of Android, the servers had to be shut down. Losing server support is a huge deal for cloud apps. A server shutdown initiates the crashing of the app – either it fails to start or it simply displays a blank screen. In the end, earlier versions of Android were transformed to empty husks, devoid of any cloud support; forever erased in the books of technology history... until Google saved the day.

The Milestone 3

Android first appeared in public as the m3-rc20a, where m3 stands for Milestone 3 also known as the Android 0.5.

The interview conducted by BusinessWeek with Andy Rubin, confirms that as early as 2003, this Android co-founder had foresight by predicting that smart gadgets will be the next big trend in the tech industry. He believes that development of smarter hand-held devices has tremendous potential especially if the owner's location and personal preferences can be integrated into it. This explains Android's shift from targeting digital cameras to mobile phones; attracting tech giant Google who aims to have a foot in the door of mobile gadgets.

In August 2005, Google quietly bought the 22-month old start-up, named the Android Inc., a Palo Alto-based company co-founded by Rich Miner, Chris White and Nick Sears along with Andy Rubin. While there was much speculation on Google's move to develop a mobile device operating system, nothing much was discussed about the newly acquired company except that it makes software for mobile phones. Furthermore, Google's spokesperson declined to elaborate on the intricacies of the deal and only stated that they are ecstatic about the tremendous talent and technology brought by the people behind Android Inc.

Two years later, **November 2007** marks a milestone for Google and the newly formed Open Handset Alliance – a group of over eighty mobile operators, software companies and handset manufacturers aiming to accelerate mobile tech development through the open platform. Launching Android as their very first product, it became the first and only open OS that eventually overtook iOS seven years later. Back then, the Milestone 3 was still running on emulators and was immediately dismissed as another Blackberry clone. And while it was just released hot off the racks, many ironically perceived it as just another old interface. It did not make a great impression to say the least.

The Milestone 3 had some touch screen support for a few features yet it was still primarily controlled through a 5-way d-pad. At this early stage though, animations are already supported by Android: for instance, an icon grows or shrinks as it enters or exits the dock center window.

Notifications were indicated by a smiley face and the only way to access the notification is to press 'up' on the d-pad while you are at your home screen. Upon opening the notification, the status bar expands slightly and the text appears encased in a speech bubble.

From Left to Right: The Milestone 3 Home sreen, the Navigation Panel, and the Applications Drawer

Source: http://arstechnica.com/gadgets/2014/06/building-android-a-40000-word-history-of-googles-mobile-os/

Aside from that, multitasking is another feature supported by Milestone 3. If you open an app, it would save its current state rather than shut itself down. It was a feature that Apple's iOS struggled with until the iOS 4 release in 2010.

Unlike in the exclusive platform model adopted by Apple, wherein the development pace was set internally by the organization, Android's open platform model set a faster pace in the app development field, despite numerous trial and errors especially during the initial stages. With the Milestone 3 release, the long journey for the Android evolution begins.

The Milestone 5

Google released a majorly overhauled interface three months after the debut of Milestone 3. Dubbed as the m5-rc14 or the Milestone 5, it broke away from the Blackberry template and adapted a more finger-friendly format.

Although it was still named as the Android 0.5, many of the core features of modern Android versions are rooted in this one version. While every component was ready for public release – menu, notification panel, overall layout, the home screen was one major feature that needed improvement. On a single-screen wallpaper, you will find the dock and app drawer seated on the main screen. Upon selection of the app drawer , you will see an "all" button located at the lower-right portion of the screen. Selecting this button displays the app list on the left side of the page. The Dialer and Contacts menu were located right above this 'all' button. Moving upwards, you will find four blocks where the recently accessed apps can be found. Overall, it had minimum app selection. While it looked functional on the emulator, it doesn't seem to work on an actual device.

Left to right: The homescreen; homescreen with app list on the left side

Source: http://arstechnica.com/gadgets/2014/06/building-android-a-40000-word-history-of-googles-mobile-os/2/

Included in the Milestone 5 is Google's first attempt in creating a dialer. Each button block was shaded with a white fill and upon closer inspection, you will notice that the numbers are vertically misaligned; occupying most of the top portion of the block. Upon typing, the numbers appear in a separate gradient-filled bar where a speech bubble enclosed x is located on its right side, acting as the backspace button. Needless to say, it looked bizzare, as if it had been lifted from another interface and edited to capture only the essential functions. Furthermore, the absence of the dial button on the touch-screen interface, limits the capacity of the user to make calls from the dialer. Handsets running on Milestone 5 needed a separate dial button on the actual hardware to facilitate ease of making phone calls.

The Dialer Page of Milestone 5

Source: http://arstechnica.com/gadgets/2014/06/building-android-a-
40000-word-history-of-googles-mobile-os/2/

The highlight of the Milestone 5 is the notifications panel. As in any current smartphone model, the notifications panel can be pulled from the top of the screen to display a list of the latest alerts. Each notification can be selected and opens the corresponding app for it.

The icons, artwork and overall look of the Milestone 5 was refreshing. With the icons sporting a cartoony look it was a clear indication of Google's intent to break away from its previously dry, Blackberry-inspired interface. In the notification panel for instance, the white, cornered icons were edited to show rounded edges with a light-green fill. Although there are still unusual choices evident in the interface, like a black underline included with the signal bar (shown above), the Milestone 5 is a major step in the development of better Android versions.

The Android 0.9: Beta

August 2008, Google unveiled another iteration of its Android OS, the Android 0.9 and called it Beta. Packed with full-color features, every app seems to pop out of its new desktop-style home screen. The once bare Milestone 5 home screen gained a full menu set that included a search button, a setting option and even a lock screen. Its menu design became the default design for the succeeding versions until Android 2.3 came with a revamped look.

While additional apps such as Messaging, Alarm clock and Music were introduced by Google in Beta, Apple was busy launching their App Store and were taking third-party submissions by then. In addition, they've already released the iPhone 3G, iPhone's second generation handset that came with an upgraded iOS, a month ahead of Android 0.9. Given the scenario, it seemed that Google is way behind and needs to speed up to stay in the game.

The App Drawer Page of Beta

Source: http://arstechnica.com/gadgets/2014/06/building-android-a-40000-word-history-of-googles-mobile-os/3/

From Milestone 5, all the artwork had to be redone to come up with a sleeker looking OS version. Hence, Android 0.9 came with a completely customizable main screen where apps and widgets can be dragged out of the drawer to your preferred location. All you have to do is to pull up the app drawer from the bottom of the screen and choose an app. Apply long press on the icon until you can move it across the main screen. In case your list of frequently used apps changes, you can delete any unused shortcuts by long pressing the icon and dragging it towards a trashcan icon on the main screen.

Android 0.9 was equipped with three widgets: search, clock and picture frame. The search widget features a text box for the user to type in any keyword or phrase pertaining to the information needed. When the Go button is hit, the browser launches on screen. Back then, the search widget had the same icon as the picture frame.

One of the interesting features of the wallpaper option was the Purchased Pictures icon. Whether Google was planning to gain profit from wallpapers or thinking of including a carrier, no one knows. It was just there. Now, its absence from the current interface serves as evidence that the company did not pursue the idea.

Android 0.9 stands as a reminder that Google was not foremost a design company. Much of the work on Android0.9 were contracted to other companies during those times. An example is the clock widget with the word MALMO written on it. This text actually refers to the hometown of The Astonishing Tribe, a design firm famous for creating interactive user interface for various devices.

Despite that, it showed a lot of potential. It was the Android version with a lot of firsts: first version that supported Google Maps; first to carry the Messaging app; first to have a music app; and finally first to carry a copy-paste feature. When you long press a text box, a dialog box appears asking you to either save or recall any text on the clipboard. It was not until two years later that iOS had this feature.

Dialer and incoming call screen comparison between Beta and Milestone 5

Source: http://arstechnica.com/gadgets/2014/06/building-android-a-40000-word-history-of-googles-mobile-os/4/

Furthermore, Android 0.9's dialer had an improved look as well. All the quirkiness and misalignment issues that were prominent in Milestone 5's dialer were replaced with professional looking graphics. A normal backspace button appeared in place of the speech bubble button while the white number blocks were replaced with black circular buttons. Every character was perfectly centered within the buttons including the pound and asterisk keys. What's more, dialing on the number display starts a call. This is quintessential in doing away with the "call" and "end" hardware keys integrated into several Android handsets. Overall, functionality significantly improved although a little more tweaking is necessary.

Android 1.0

The first actual version of Android, Android 1.0, was launched in October 2008. Before that, the beta SDK (Software Development Kit) for Android was released in 2007. Android 1.0 debuted on the T-Mobile G1 also known as the HTC Dream. With Apple's iPhone 3G and Nokia's 1680 classic selling more than 30 millions units each since their launch, HTC Dream running on Android 1.0 lagged behind significantly. In fact, it took half a year (April 2009) before they hit the 1 million mark in total units sold.

The G1 featured 256MB of storage; single-core 528mHz processor and 192 MB of RAM. It has a 3.2 inch screen mounted on a sliding mechanism that when pushed upwards, reveals a keyboard equipped with fifty buttons. While it has almost every imaginable hardware control: track ball, camera shutter button, volume adjuster, etc, it lacked the press coverage and smoothness present in iPhones. Still it was the first time Android was actually running on a hardware instead of a snail-paced emulator.

The interface looked similar to the Android 0.9 released in the past two months, although Android 1.0's consumer product showed more variety in terms of the available apps. By bringing along the full suite of Google apps in its interface, users were given access to Youtube, calendar, gmail, voice dialer and market all in one place. The most significant feature of the Android 1.0 was the Android Market Beta which initially housed apps and games. Google's vision for this market is to be a place where customers can find everything they need for their Android gadgets including OS updates.

At the time of Android 1.0's launch, Apple's App Store has been running in full swing for four months already. Despite that, Google still had one major advantage. With the open platform scheme implemented in the Android Market, developers for the Android store are given freedom to do anything, even replacing stock apps. This accelerated the development of various stock apps alongside tons of other third-party apps. Meanwhile, apps for iPhones were subjected to stringent quality control and stock app duplication checks.

This lack-of-control strategy became a double edged sword for Android's evolution. On one hand, it encouraged innovation among developers to create even better versions of the stock apps.

On the other hand, quality is at risk since users are also likely to access trashy apps in the store.

The Android Market Interface

Source: http://android-developers.blogspot.com/2008/08/android-market-user-driven-content.html

Although the Android Market no longer communicates with Google servers today, it was among the early apps documented online. Switching to its main screen gives you access to common areas such as My Downloads, Search and Games. The top portion featured the latest apps in a horizontal scrolling display. When you go through the search results or your downloaded apps, the page will display a scroll down list that features the name, rating, cost and the developer of the app. If you go through the individual app pages, you will find a short description of the app including the total number of installations, customer comments and more importantly, the install button. At this point, the Android Market only has a 500-character decription box where developers can showcase their creations. Pictures were not yet supported at this time which made maintaining a changelog quite challenging.

At the onset, the Android Market has been showing permission requirements needed by an app prior to installation. This was something that Apple was not able to implement until 2012, when the Path app was found to upload entire contents of address books to cloud storage without the user's consent and worse, their awareness. While the permissions display gave a full list of information that the app needs to access, Android's permission alert lead users towards agreeing. An OK button can be chosen if you agree with the terms yet there was no exsisting cancel button. You have to press the back button to cancel the installation.

Other notable features of Android 1.0 were the Voice dialer, a pattern lock screen, time setter and the low battery warning.

In terms of functionality, a lot of work still needs to be done: the operability of Android devices still relies heavily on hardware buttons; auto-rotate is yet to be added; and built-in app updates still have to be integrated into the existing app store. However, for a pilot OS version such as the Android 1.0, it was a good attempt.

Android 1.1

In February 2009, the first public update arrived. Named as the Android 1.1, it featured minor changes in the four and half months old Andoid 1.0. It had the Google voice search, a cloud-supported voice activated search, which opens a Google search page after you speak. Aside from that, the Android Market now included paid apps. With the sorting screen you can exclusively browse free apps, paid apps or a mix of the two. For Maps, the Google Latitude allowed users to share their location with friends. Lastly, there was a System updates option included in the About Phone screen wherein users can access the latest information and of course updates for their current OS version.

Android 1.5 Cupcake

Codename: Cupcake. Three months after the 1.1 release, Android 1.5 certainly made its mark in the history of Android. Aside from being the first carrier of a codename, it did not fall short in terms of its features.

Among the highlights of Cupcake is the on-screen keyboard. This paved the way for the development of a slate-styled Android device minus the numerous hardware keys and the slide mechanism. It had a caps lock key enabling the user to switch in between the lowercase and uppercase characters. The lowercase letter was the default setting but there is an option for turning it off in the suggestion bar found just above the keyboard. Aside from letter options, switching between numbers and punctuations is possible as well. Long pressing the period key for instance, opens up more punctuation choices.

Third party widgets were another core feature of Cupcake, that became central to Android's interface until today. The smart thing about it is that developers can bundle apps with the home screen widget. Of course, Google first showed a few widgets of its own that came with the Music and Calendar apps.

Google's Calendar and Music Widgets in the Home Screen

Source: http://arstechnica.com/gadgets/2014/06/building-android-a-40000-word-history-of-googles-mobile-os/8/

Zoom controls became system-wide in Cupcake. Two rectangle halves with rounded corners served as the new zoom controls replacing the big circles used previously. The size of the gallery, browser, and Google Maps can be controlled with these overhauled zoom feature. The browser for instance, had variations when it comes to zooming functions. With the 1x button, users can return to the basic zoom level after zooming out or in.

Building on the copy-paste feature of the Android 1.0, Cupcake enabled users to copy blocks of text from an existing webpage in addition to the current copy feature applicable in the Messaging app. Choosing *copy text* from the menu activates the highlight mode. With this option, you will be able to highlight the text you need to copy by simply dragging your finger over the content of interest. If you lift your finger off the screen, Android will copy the selected text and remove the highlight automatically. Therefore, you need precision to capture important text. This is where G1's trackball came in handy.

As for the lock screens - both for the default and pattern-activated versions, the once empty black backgrounds were transformed into a backdrop that carries the same wallpaper as that of the homescreen. Unfortunately, the lighter background revealed the messy work on the pattern lock screen, wherein the white dots were slightly off-center within enclosing black circle.

Android 1.6 Donut

In previous versions, pressing on the search button from the home screen of your phone will always bring you to an online search page. The release of Android 1.6, Donut introduced the phone search to customers along with major improvements in the Camera app, the Android Market and battery monitoring.

With Donut, the built-in camera app is expected have better responsiveness. Launching speed is 39% faster than before and the lag time in between camera shoots has been decreased by 28%. The most noticeable feature is the overall interface. From a full screen design, it transformed into a box viewfinder with controls on the right side much like a classic camera. Reviewing photos taken is a breeze with the image viewer. You will no longer be taken to the gallery just to do a quick review of the photo. Aside from that, the camera controls changed to picture controls once you are in the image viewer screen. You can now delete, share or use photos as wallpaper.

The much needed update of the Android Market was seen after the launch of Donut. The previously dull, all-black design was changed to a white and green combo, somehow alluding to the Android mascot.

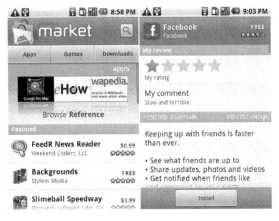

The Android Market in Donut

Source: http://arstechnica.com/gadgets/2014/06/building-android-a-40000-word-history-of-googles-mobile-os/9/#donut

Upon opening the market's home screen, you will find a banner where the "Android Market" is written, with emphasis on the word "market". A search button is located to the right of the name to facilitate ease of browsing through thousands of apps. Below this banner, you will see separate buttons for downloads, games and apps. You will also find the featured apps neatly arranged in a vertical scrolling list.

The most significant improvement of the market is the integration of app screenshots. Finally, Android users can catch a glimpse of any app interface prior to installation. Before, users depend on fellow Android user reviews and the 500-word description uploaded by the developer. Now, they can see the app for themselves before deciding to download and install it. Although it involved more work – browsing through the screenshots required a bit of scrolling, you need to check the reviews to assess the app, etc. the availability of screenshots was definitely helpful.

Battery life has been a limitation in the use of Android phones even before. Google's answer is the battery monitoring app made available with Donut. Simply access the "About Phone" menu and search for the "Battery use" option. Here, you will find the most power-consuming app or hardware function since the battery usage is displayed in percentage. If you tap on an item, you will be brought to a separate page where you can view some relevant statistics. What's more, you have the option to stop the app from running to save on battery power. You can also use the data to alert developers to tweak their products to consume lesser energy.

Other features of Donut include:

- **Text-to-speech engine** – wherein both apps and the operating system can talk back to the user with a robot voice. With the Speech synthesizer, you can even customize the default language or set the speech rate.

- **Location-based search and the Voice search** – With the phone search capability brought by Donut, you can easily find relevant content on your mobile device. Google made it even more exciting with the Voice search app. Thus, if you want to call a friend, simply press the voice search button and say "call Ana mobile" and your device will comply promptly. The downside though is its vulnerability to errors particularly when used in noisy environments.

Another Google breakthrough in searching is the integration of location information so that users can find more relevant content. For instance, typing "Italian restaurant" will result to a list of the most popular Italian food joints within your locality.

- **Better display resolution support** – While most Android end-users may care less about resolution support, it matters most to several app developers. Resolution support refers to the correct scaling of apps according to screen size. Today, a plethora of mobile handsets exist, each with a corresponding screen size. Thus, resolution support becomes an indispensable upgrade particularly for many app developers today.

Android 2.0 Éclair

October 2009 – Only forty-one days after the release of Donut, Google unveiled the Motorola Droid, the first-ever second generation Android handset running on the Éclair.

Android Programming In a Day!

The Motorola Droid

Source: https://skatter.com/2009/12/quick-look-android-2-0-1-on-motorola-droid/

The launch of Google's second generation phone did brought significant improvements in terms of functionality and style. Yet, the most memorable part of it all was the flamboyant campaign preceeding its release. Droid was not just another competing handset for the iPhone. It was also chosen as the flagship device for Verizon Wireless, the largest telecommunications provider in the United States, with over 90 million subscribers in 2009. For this reason, Verizon poured money into the Droid's marketing campaigns. Starting with the licensing of the word 'droid' from Lucasfilm, the campaign eventually resulted to the production of a series of loud and explosion-filled commercials in order to position the Droid as one kick-ass alternative to the iPhone.

Hardware upgrades are evident in the Droid. Although the sliding mechanism and actual keyboard were still present, it had a more streamlined look. Motorola ditched the trackball but retained the 5-way d-pad and placed it beside the hardware keyboard. On the glass touchscreen, capacitive-touch buttons were painted neatly on one edge. Users can now switch between the hardware buttons and the capacitive-touch buttons while navigating the device. Compared to the HTC Dream, it had a bigger 3.7 inch LCD; 256MB of internal storage; single-core 550mHz processor; and

256 MB of RAM. Aside from that, it also had a running GPS navigation tool that gives turn-by-turn instructions to help users reach their target destinations.

The Android Éclair Interface

Source: http://devilshouts.com/android-version-history/

Éclair paved the way for the development of Android devices without the hardware buttons "end" and "call". It also brought elements of grunge to its interface. The default wallpaper that features a calm, water oasis was replaced by an image of dirty concrete. A red, pulsing camera eye served as the boot animation while the default email alert tone was a voice screaming out 'DRRRROOOOOIIDDD'. You could think of it as Google's angsty-goth-teenager phase.

The Arc Unlock Feature

Source: https://skatter.com/2009/12/quick-look-android-2-0-1-on-motorola-droid/

Major changes are evident in the homescreen. For instance, the clock widget in Donut was replaced with a search widget. You will also find the Messaging app and Android Market app in the layout along with the dialer, contacts, browser, and maps apps.

The Éclair came with a brand new lock screen. Since the slide-to-unlock feature is already patented by Apple, Google decided to go with an arc unlock gesture. If you put your thumb on the lock icon and slide it towards the right, you phone will unlock. In contrast, putting your thumb on the volume icon and sliding it towards the left silences the phone.

Overall, the Éclair boasts of improved capabilities in accounts management, contacts and sync. The new account manager API allows users to manage multiple accounts in a single device, enabling them to keep track of messages and updates sent to their social media or communication accounts (such as emails) thoughout the day. Any new incoming message goes to the combined inbox page wherein users can view all of the latest messages from all their accounts in one page. For the contacts app, the "Quick Contact" is a new feature that lets you choose the most convenient way to communicate with your peers. When you tap on a contact number, a single menu bar containing various communication icons appears. You can choose to email or IM your colleague depending on convenience.

The Éclair's Quick Contacts Feature

Source: http://developer.android.com/about/versions/android-2.0-highlights.html#PlatformTechnologies

Other features of the Éclair include:

- **Message search function** – that enabled users to find important MMS or SMS stored in the Inbox;

- **Auto deletion** of the oldest messages in a thread when the set message limit is reached;

- **New Camera features** – which include a built-in flash support, macro focus, scene mode, digital zoom, color effect and white balance; and lastly,

- **Bluetooth support** which enabled users to connect with nearby devices and share information. This opened the doors to the development of proximity-based apps.

Android 2.1 Éclair

Only three months after the successful launch of Android 2.0, Google reached another milestone with the release of their first mobile device aptly named Nexus One. Unlike its chunky Android predecessor the G1, it had a thinner body as it ditched the hardware keyboard and sliding mechanism. Solely manufactured by HTC, it had a 3.7-inch screen; 512MB of RAM; 1 GHz single core processor; and 512MB of internal storage.

This new handset came with the Android 2.1 OS, still named Éclair, that contains mostly huge interface changes, aimed to grab any Android users' attention.

Live wallpapers were among the main features of Android 2.1. These are essentially moving images that can be set as the home screen's background. The default wallpaper is an array of small squares where streaks of yellow, blue, green and red lights continuously pass across it. Among the choices were swirling images that shift in accordance to your tapping motion or the music currently playing. While these moving wallpapers were amusing to watch, it consumed power and slowed down the phone.

With Android 2.1, additional home screens reached up to five pages, where you can fill each with your frequently used apps. Furthermore, a thumbnail navigation system was added to allow you to switch easily from one screen to the other. Swiping to the right or left will still bring you to every homescreen, however the thumbnail navigation system gives you a peek into all five screens simultaneously. Directly tapping one of the screens will bring you straight to your chosen home page.

Android 2.2 Froyo

March 2010 – Four months after the Android 2.1 release came Froyo. With the name change, users can expect major improvements that focused on device speed.

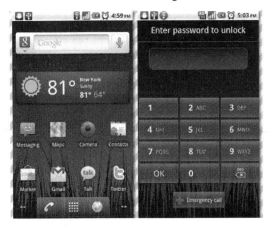

The Froyo's Homescreen and Lock Screen

Source: http://gizmodo.com/5549260/android-22-review

Upon reaching the home screen, a translucent navigation bar welcomes you providing easy access to the browser, app tray and dialer. Even Google's search bar underwent some modifications to allow web searching and phone searching. You will also find two new widgets in the interface. One is the helper widget that gives quick tips on how to manage and navigate the home screen and the other one is the Android Market widget displaying a slideshow of the most downloaded apps. New wallpapers or alert tones were absent in Froyo.

Since Android 2.1, the settings page for Froyo was tweaked to incorporate a separate Display settings page. Check the Wireless and Network settings page and you will find a newly added option: USB tethering and Wireless Hotspot. The USB tethering option enables you to connect your smartphone to a desktop computer through the USB port. On the other hand, the Wireless Hotspot option allows you to share your mobile phone's 3G or GPRS connection, through Wifi, to other nearby handheld devices. In the Application settings page, you will also find a task manager that lets you quit unused apps manually to save some battery power and RAM. In addition, there is a cool back-up feature that lets you to store any application data on any Google server. In case you accidentally reset your phone settings, you can be sure that any of your stored app data can be retrieved. For developers, there is an option that allows the user to move apps from the device's internal memory to an external storage such as the SD card. While this can help users free up some internal memory space, it may not work on all apps since it is a developer-enabled feature. Lastly, the lock screen now features the password or PIN support to provide alternatives to the pattern key.

While the new Just-In-Time (JIT) compiler run significantly faster than that used in Éclair, Froyo was still less responsive and smooth than the iOS. Yet, memory management and multitasking improved overall in comparison to past Android OS versions.

Android 2.3 Gingerbread

Gingerbread's Home Screen

Source: http://www.anandtech.com/show/4050/a-busy-day-for-android-nexus-s-and-gingerbread-23-officially-announced

December 2010 – Android 2.3 debuted on the Nexus S which was solely manufactured by Samsung. By this time, Apple had already launched the iPhone 4 along with the updated iOS 4 that features Facetime and multitasking support. Meanwhile, Microsoft made a comeback in November 2010 with the release of the Windows 7 smartphone.

Gingerbread was packed with updated user features aimed to improve functionality, speed and overall aesthetic value. The gray-shaded notification bar, for instance, was changed into solid black shade while menu options were tweaked to have either a white or green color. Black pixels is one way to leverage power saving, particularly in devices with AMOLED display. With the multi-touch virtual keyboard, high speed texting is a cinch as the keys have been repositioned to facilitate ease of typing. Also, long pressing each key opens up a menu of special characters that you can use as well. The copy-paste support works without a trackball.

Applying long press on a word activates the word selection handles that you can adjust manually to select all the relevant information.

Significant improvements in battery power management and application control is evident in Gingerbread. A graph of power usage, since the time the device was turned on, can be viewed in the battery settings page. Here, you will be able to see the energy consumption of every process in percentage. What's more, charge events and screen on events are clearly marked in the graph. For the applications control, a link has been added in the options menu to connect it to the applications setting page where you can see various active apps and check the corresponding memory footprint.

Android 3.0 Honeycomb

February 2011 – Honeycomb was Google's rushed answer to Apple's iPad, lauched ten months prior. At the Dive Into Mobile event, Andy Rubin appeared with a tablet on hand. It was revealed later that the device was the Motorola Xoom – a 10-inch tablet with dual core 1 GHz processor and 1 GB of RAM, the flagship device for the Android tablet OS, the Honeycomb.

Source code for the half-baked OS was never released to the public primarily because Google did not want to pressure app developers to support a half-broken system. At the launch, problems appeared one by one: support for Adobe Flash was missing; SD cards cannot be read; and the overall interface was unstable. Despite that, the framework and interface were rebuilt in the succeeding months to come up with a more cohesive and efficient OS.

Sci-fi immediately comes to mind with the new homescreen. A notification bar can be found on the lower right corner of the screen while on the left, there are three buttons that allow you to go one page back; go to the home screen; or check the multitasking UI. At the top portion, you will find the search bar, application tray, and an add button for exporting widgets, shortcuts and other items to the homescreen.

Honeycomb Homescreen

Source: http://www.anandtech.com/show/4189/google-android-30-honeycomb-preview

The notification panel was hidden at the lower-right corner of the screen; displaying only the essentials, such as the remaining battery power and time, when on standby mode. Clicking the notification panel opens a window that shows the current system status and provides access to various display settings such as screen orientation and brightness. The overhaul included more detail in notifications. Alerts from the Music Player app for instance, showed album art while the Google Talk app displayed photos or message preview.

In Honeycomb, users saw the Action Bar widget as the replacement of the Title Bar found on top of very action window within an app. Settings and options are displayed depending on the activity to be done. If you're using the Gmail app, you will notice that selecting a message transforms the Action Bar such that it displays the following options: report spam, mark as starred, mark as unread, and change labels. For the copy-paste activity, press holding a text launches the Select feature wherein the copy, paste, share and cut options are easily accessed in the Action Bar.

Fragments is a feature that allows developers to conceptualize more flexible UI tailored for tablet screens. Larger-sized screens allow ease of combination or interchangeabiity of UI elements. It lets a developerbreakdown every activity into several fragments. Take the Pulse app as an example. A phone with a smaller screen considers viewing a list as one activity and reading one article another activity. In fragments, these two activities can be merged into one action whereby one fragment shows the acticle list while the other fragment shows the chosen article to be read. Every fragment has a corresponding set of user input events and callback methods. Overall, fragments are modular, reusable and adaptable to various screen sizes.

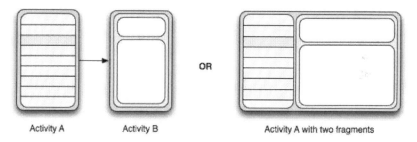

| Activity A | Activity B | | Activity A with two fragments |

Working with Fragments

Source: http://www.anandtech.com/show/4189/google-android-30-honeycomb-preview

When it comes to hardware, the most significant change is the multi-core support for the Dalvik VM environment. This allows leveraging of processing power to speed up acitivities and promote better battery life. This is a step towards changing the overall performance of tablets in the future.

Android 4.0 Ice Cream Sandwich

Left to Right: The Ice Cream Sandwich Lock Screen and Home Screen

Source: http://developer.android.com/about/versions/android-4.0-
highlights.html#UserFeatures

October 2011 – The Ice Cream Sandwich OS debuted on both smartphones and tablets and was once more made open source. This upgrade is a huge deal particularly for phones still stuck on the Gingerbread version for almost a year. Essentially, Android 4.0 brought the Honeycomb experience to smaller handheld devices; now mobile phone users can see firsthand the action bar, on-screen buttons and a brand new design language on their very own handsets.

The Ice Cream Sandwich is conceptualized to work without hardware buttons. On the bottom of the screen, you will find the System bar filled with three softkeys arranged in the following order (from right to left): Recent Apps, Home and Back. The recent apps or multi-tasking key was adopted from the Honeycomb UI, where it showed a set of thumbnails showing your recently opened apps. The cool part about it is that swiping sideaways shuts down the chosen app, and saves some precious battery power. Pressing the Home buttons brings you back to the main screen while pressing Back leads you to a previously viewed page.

Text input and spell checking is made faster with the soft keyboard. Through the default dictionary, suggested words come out as you type and a display of relevant words is shown in a strip from which you can choose the right term. The spellchecker feature helps you locate misspelled words by underlining errors and shows a list of suggested replacements. With a single tap, the user can select replacement suggestions; delete words; or add words to the dictionary.

Building on the previous voice search engine, the voice input engine allows you to dictate words continuously with its streaming voice recognition support. Users can say what they want to say, for as long as they like using their preferred language. What's more, punctuations can also be dictated to come up with correct sentences. You can even pause to catch your breath without interrupting the whole process. Dictation errors are underlined in gray so that users can locate them easily for quick correction using suggested replacement words.

Other features include:

- **Face Unlock** – that allows users to unlock their handsets with their own faces. This feature maximizes the use of the front-facing camera in tandem with the face recognition technology to register a face upon setup and upon unlocking the device. With face recognition, users simply hold the device before their faces to gain access to their gadget. This is a refreshing alternative to the existing PIN entry or pattern recognition used in earlier versions of the lock screen.

- **Live effects for more interesting videos** – With this feature, graphical transformations can now be integrated in your captured videoclips for added humor and personality. Backgrounds can be changed to any custom image (example: a raging volcano or the vast galaxy) prior to shooting the video. In addition to that, Silly Faces covers a wide range of morphing effects that utilize GPU filters and face recognition to change various facial features. Whether you prefer small eyes or a squeezed face, you can integrate all that effects not just within the Camera app but also in video chats.

Essentially, Ice Cream Sandwich's debut marks the beginning of Android's contemporary age. Google's intent to become better in software design was showcased in this version through the elegant and sleek interface filled with smart built-in features for ease of use. Indeed, Android has come a long way and finally pays attention to the finer details.

Android 4.1, 4.2, 4.3: Jellybean

July 2012 – marks the release of Android 4.1 named the Jellybean. Since then, Google settled into a six –month interval between new Android version releases, giving OEMs an opportunity to catch their breaths before jumping to the next project.

Integral to Google's leap with Android 4.1 is Project Butter. It was the name given to the deliberate effort of the company's engineers to make all Android animations run seamlessly at a rate of 30 frames per second. Since scrolling ease and animation smoothness were long standing issues with the Android OS, work on its core framework and the apps eventually brought it closer to the iOS' smoothness.

Changes in the notification panel are evident. Time was displayed on the top left portion of the screen with the settings shortcut and the date. With the expandable notifications, users can now see up to eight lines of text. The buttons found at the bottom of every notification allows you to execute response actions quickly: snoozing an alarm; making a return call from a missed call alert; or sharing a text through social media accounts.

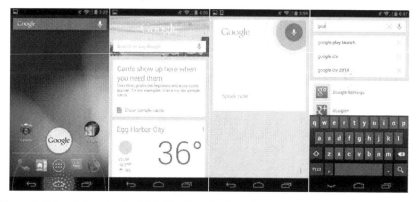

From left to right: Android 4.1's Google Search App, the Google Now cards, voice-activated search, and the well-known text search

Source: http://arstechnica.com/gadgets/2014/06/building-android-a-40000-word-history-of-googles-mobile-os/21/

Android 4.1 also came with a the latest version of the Google Search app. Introduced as the "Google Now", it displayed a set of cards found just below the search bar, that contains suggested search results that Google thinks are relevant to you. Examples include calendar appointment locations, recently searched places in Google Maps, weather forecasts, and the time at your homeland in case you are on the road in a different location.

Launching the new search app can be done with a swipe from the System bar or by tapping on the Google icon. By applying long press on the System bar, a ring appears and works in the same manner as the lock screen ring. Text boxes called "Cards" scroll vertically and can be swiped away in case you don't want to view them. For the Voice search, queries are not just blindly accepted by Google. If it had an available answer, Google will talk back through the Text-to-Speech engine. Old-school text searches are still available and can be executed simply by typing the content in the search box.

Starting out as an online search engine, Google positioned its revamped search app in Android 4.1 as the future of searching application. By putting all their data mining knowledge to work, they have created an efficient and effective tool that overthrew rivals like Bing.

November 2012 – Four months after the first iteration of Jellybean, Google released minor OS updates in the Android 4.2 version. Along with the OS launch came the introduction of two flagship devices: Nexus 4 and Nexus 10, both sold directly by Google through the Play Store.

Nexus 4 is a handset that boasts of a 4.7-inch LCD; a quadcore 1.5 GHz processor; and 2GB of RAM. Solely manufactured by LG, the handset showed a better form molded from high-class materials such as glass. Unfortunately, the lack of LTE became a huge impediment to its use at a time when faster modems proliferated. Still, demand for Nexus 4 exceeded Google's targets. In fact, the unit was sold-out in less than an hour notwithstanding the Play store crash brought about by the launch rush.

Nexus 10 is the first ever 10-inch Google tablet. With its 2560x1600 display, it had the highest resolution among its contemporaries. Under the hood, you will discover that it is powered by a dual core, 1.7GHz processor with 2GB RAM. While tablets are typically upgraded annually, it seems that the Nexus 10 is more likely to stay as it is in the coming months. Google's 7-inch tablets are doing well on the other hand and it seems like they are leaving their partner companies to explore the tablet market.

Android 4.2's lockscreen, wallpaper and clock widget

Source: http://arstechnica.com/gadgets/2014/06/building-android-a-40000-word-history-of-googles-mobile-os/22/

Much of the updates can be seen in the multiple lock screen that can house various widgets according to the user's preference. Aside from the old-school analog clock, users can now select an email widget or the calendar widget, and display it on a separate screen based on frequency of use or personal aesthetic.

Another significant addition brought by 4.2 is the Quick settings panel. While Honeycomb enabled users to quickly tweak power settings in the tablet, 4.2 Jellybean brought this experience to smartphones. In the Quick settings page, users can check on the status of their battery power; adjust brightness of the screen; or view network connections.

July 2013 – marks the launch of the almost insignificant update, the Android 4.3. Why insignificant? In between the release of 4.2 and 4.3, updates for Gmail, Music, and Games among others were uploaded in the Play Store. Packaging everything into 4.3 could have been a better option. In any case, it contained minor updates for items that cannot be upgraded through the store.

Wearability is one of the themes for 4.3. With support for the Bluetooth Low Energy, users can now have a way to connect wirelessly to other Android devices using minimal battery power. Another addition was the Notification Access API that enabled apps to replicate the content and take control over the notification panel. While this feature may seem redundant given the notification panel, this function is more useful for checking alerts in any external device aside from your phone.

Needless to say, the 4.3 launch was less exciting given that updates can be accessed through the Play Store. On a more positive note, the increased modularity of the Android OS enables Google to upload recent updates in the Play Store as they are completed, allowing improvements to take place gradually instead of dropping everything in one OS version.

Android 4.4 Kitkat

October 31, 2013 – Google picked Halloween to aptly launch the Android 4.4 dubbed as Kitkat. Their team up with Nestle led to an exciting campaign where limited-edition Android-Shaped bars were made available to the public.

Nexus 5 was the chosen device for Kitkat. It had a 5-inch display; a 2.3 GHz processor; and 2GB RAM. The Play Store was again chosen as its selling medium. With this device, Google makes a sweet deal by positioning it as a cheaper alternative to high-end phones with similar capabilities. While a lot of phones with the given specs cost around USD600-USD700, Nexus 7 sold for USD350.

More than showcasing Google's innovation skills as seen in the Ice Cream Sandwich release, Kitkat became a marketing strategy to expand Android's reach across the high-end and low-end markets.

Kitkat's advantage over previous Android OS versions is its lower memory usage. Through the Project Svelte, optimization work were done one after the other to come up with an Android OS that can run seamlessly on at least 340MB of RAM. In the developing world, devices mostly ran on 512MB of RAM. Tapping into this fast-growing market calls for the development of an OS with lower memory requirements. The advanced UI of Ice Cream Sandwich unfortunately raised system requirements leaving tons of newly launched low-end handsets running on Gingerbread.

Minor design changes can be observed in the overall interface of Kitkat. Although there was a new home screen that can only be seen on Nexus 5, at least for the first months after release. This new home screen was named the Google Now Launcher which was originally the Google Search app. This launcher can be accessed by swiping from the leftmost home screen aside from swiping up from the system bar. It had a more integrated look and functionality as well. Some card designs were cleaned and an updated set of buttons at the bottom led to help, reminders, feedback, and customization options. The interface veered away from the black background by adopting transparency in the app drawer and home screen. Furthermore, folders now had a white background to achieve a brighter look.

Android 5.0 Lollipop

June 25, 2014 – During the Google I/O Conference, the Android 5.0 was released. Named as the Lollipop, it gave the previous OS versions a much needed facelift, since the Ice Cream Sandwich launch.

The Lollipop Homescreen with the Calendar and Search Widgets

Source: http://www.knowyourmobile.com/mobile-phones/android-50-lollipop/22337/android-lollipop-review-new-features-design-detailed

You might have heard of the relentless mention of Material Design in various Lollipop review and discussions. Essentially, material design refers to Google's set of design principles governing the company's approach to improving various services across numerous plaforms. From the home screen to the tiny notification button, everything looks different in comparison to previous Android versions. What's exciting about it, aside from the fresh aesthetics, is its responsiveness to touch. In most cases, pressing any button shows a light shade radiating outward to indicate that the device has already registered your touch.

A notable improvement in Notifications is the addition of a notification alert in the lock screen. Every alert comes in a card that can be swiped downwards to expand the notification. You can also swipe it away or tap on it to open the appropriate app after unlocking the screen. Privacy protection is now enabled by controlling what the notification reveals. Furthermore, the priority mode allows you choose what types of notifications will ring your device.

For multitasking, Google replaced Recent Apps with the Overview menu. Instead of sticking with the list format, running apps are displayed as a stack of cards wherein scrolling through the stack allows you to switch in-between apps faster. If you want to compose a new email and check your inbox from time to time, you will see two tabs for Gmail, one for each activity.

With two other competitors in the mobile industry market, Google certainly took the right step by focusing on their design and in the process making the Android standout. At this point, choosing a handset is not just about the OS. More importantly, it is about selecting that right device that caters to your needs. Lollipop came out not just with a polished design but also with new features that certainly boosts functionality.

The following infographics takes you through the journey of Android from being a Blackberry imitation to becoming one of the most widely used OS in the world today.

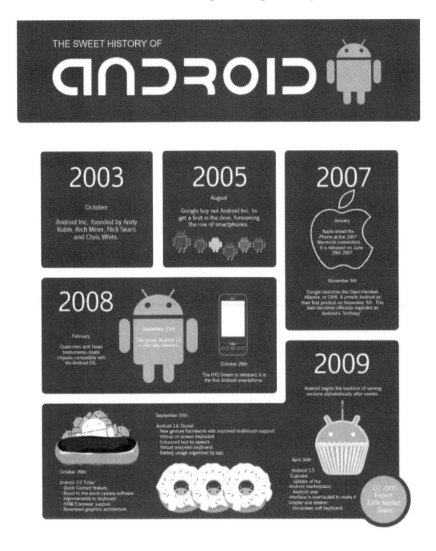

Android Programming In a Day!

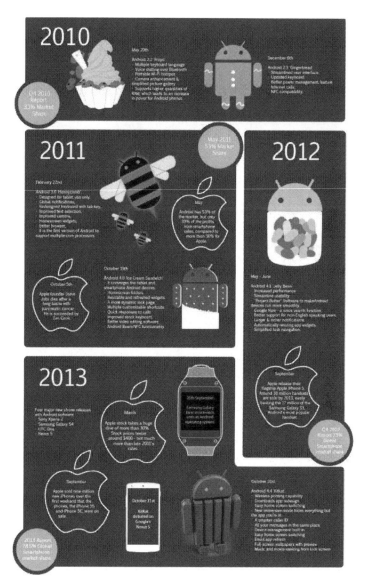

Android Through the Years

Source: http://bgr.com/2014/11/05/history-of-android-infographic/

Android by the Numbers

In 2014, Google managed to overtake Apple as the most valuable brand ending its three-year reign, according to the Millward Brown BrandZ study. Google's brand value was estimated to be around USD158 million, indicating a 40% leap from the previous year's value. On the other hand, Apple managed to achieve a 20% increase in brand value that hit over USD147 million.

The following table[1] shows that ten most valuable brands of 2014:

Rank 2014	Brand	Category	Brand Value 2014 ($M)	Brand Value Change	Rank 2013
1	Google	Technology	158,843	+40%	2
2	Apple	Technology	147,880	-20%	1
3	IBM	Technology	107,541	-4%	3
4	Microsoft	Technology	90,185	+29%	7
5	McDonald's	Fast Food	85,706	-5%	4
6	Coca-Cola	Soft Drinks	80,683	+3%	5
7	Visa	Credit Cards	79,197	+41%	9
8	AT&T	Telecoms	77,883	+3%	6
9	Marlboro	Tobacco	67,341	-3%	8
10	Amazon	Retail	64,255	+41%	14

---

[1] Source: http://www.millwardbrown.com/global-navigation/news/press-releases/full-release/2014/05/20/google-overtakes-apple-to-become-the-2014-brandz-top-100-most-valuable-global-brand

Perception was the game-changing factor in the overall result. The year 2013 stands witness to a whole slew of innovative products and strategies implemented successively by the company. From the Google Glass to the Google car, investments are being made even in aritificial intelligence, and partnerships are being forged to incorporate Android in as many products as possible. Given this scenario, consumers were able to see the capability of Google amidst the slowdown happening at Apple's camp, according to Nick Cooper, Millward Brown Optimor's Managing Director.

In less than a decade, Google managed to elevate the Android from a Blackberry clone into a powerful and independent OS embedded in more than a million devices daily. All the work done on several iterations of the Android OS finally paid off after seven years of its existence. The following[2] table provides a summary of Google's current stature in terms of global market share and revenue.

Google	Value
Google's global revenue	$66 billion
Price of Google's Motorola Mobility acquisition	$12,500 million
Android Smartphones	**Value**
Android's global market share	78.4%
Number of daily activations of Android devices	1,500,000
Global shipments of Android	1,133 million

---

[2] Source: http://www.statista.com/topics/876/android/

smartphones	
Distribution of Android Jelly Bean 4.1 x	29%
Number of Android smartphone users in the U.S.	76 million
Android Tablets	**Value**
Shipments of Android tablets worldwide	37.9 million
Android tablets global market share	36.5%
Android Apps/Google Play Store	**Value**
Number of apps downloaded from the Google Play store	50 billion
Average unique monthly users of Android's Facebook app	42.38 million
Average price of an Android app	USD 0.06

Why Android Programming is a Valuable Skill

Becoming the most valuable company in 2014 is no walk in the park. You need to consistently showcase ingenuity through your products and deliver what you promised in order to win over 75% of the global market share. Accomplishing this feat entails working with a dynamic andcreative team composed of talented and highly motivated individuals.

Given the astounding growth of Google in the past years, there's no denying that highly-skilled developers are in demand. The sudden surge of open source projects from 2010 to 2012 (as shown in the following graph), proves that there is enough reason to believe that Android's future will remain bright in the coming years.

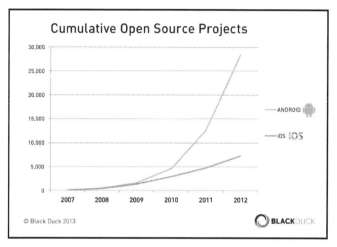

Growth of Android versus iOS from 2007 to 2012

Source: https://www.blackducksoftware.com/files/images/Cumulative-Open-Source-Mobile-Projects.png

According to Indeed, a leading job search site, Android app development is the fourth most sought-after skill in the digital industry at the moment; implying that opportunities abound for many experienced freelance developers. What's more, the pay is really good. An experienced developer makes USD100,000 annually in the United States alone.

The quickest and most accessible way to learn about Android development basics is to go online. The following list shows the most recent Android Development Courses that you can access for free.

- *Creative, Serious and Playful Science of Android Apps*: This is an introductory course featured in Coursera. The material is tailored for an audience with zero experience in programming. Starting with a discussion of fundamental computer science concepts and principles, the course gradually transitions into app building for both smartphones and tablets. By the end of the 5-week course, you are expected to create your own Android app using Google's development tools and a bit of Java. You can view announcements on the next session in Coursera.

- *Android 4 Video Bootcamp*: This course features the full recording of a 5-day camp where development for the Ice Cream Sandwich was discussed. It includes a comprehensive introductory presentation and twenty video tutorials that you can follow as you go through the learning process.

- *Building Mobile Applications with iOS, Android and HTML 5*: This is an online course offered by Harvard University last Spring of 2012. Aside from Android development lectures, HTML 5 and iOS development are also included in the series. You can also find assignments and video tutorials that will help you breeze through building your first mobile app.

While firsthand experience in using other programming languages such as C and Java is beneficial, people with no experience but with tremendous interest in coding will definitely enjoy the whole learning process. With enough focus and determination, Android app development becomes doable. Taking introductory courses on computer science is highly recommended to help newbies develop an understanding of the fundamental concepts in coding.

Android Features

Of course, for you to have a powerful application, you should know what Android is capable of. Take note that some older versions of Android may not have some of the features mentioned here. On the other hand, some of the features may not be available on certain mobile devices.

- Support Multiple Connectivity Types: WiMAX, GSM, EDGE, CDMA, IDEN, EV-DO, Bluetooth, LTE, Wi-Fi, NFC, UMTC

- Wi-Fi Direct

- Storage Type: SQLite (a relational database commonly used everywhere)

- Messaging: MMS and SMS

- Media File Type Support: H.264, H.263, AMR, MPEG0-4, AMR-WB, HE-AAC, AAC, MP3, AAC 5.1, MIDI, WAV, OGG Vorbis, BMP, PNG, GIF, JPEG

- Built in Web Browser: Supports CSS3. HTML5, and JavaScript

- Other Features: Multi Touch, Multi Language, Widgets, GCM, Wi-Fi Direct, Android Beam

Android Application Development

Android application development requires basic knowledge of the Java language. In case you are not familiar with Java, it is best that you step away from this book and learn that first. However, with basic knowledge of computer programming, you can get away without Java experience or expertise. Nevertheless, expect that you will face a very steep learning curve.

When you finish developing a program in Android, you can easily run it in your emulator or smartphone. In case you have created a useful app, you can easily upload and share or sell it on Amazon's Appstore or Google Play.

Android application development is one of the most profitable ventures in the programming development industry. As of now, Android exists on millions of mobile devices and smart appliances in the world. Truth be told, it has already outnumbered the number of computers installed with Microsoft Windows. It is also not an exaggeration that, almost every day, a million of Android powered devices is activated, as shown in the previous table.

In this book, you will learn how to create and package your own Android application. It will provide you with a step-by-step tutorial on preparing yourself and your computer for app development. And of course, the book will be sprinkled with some pro tips that can get you going in the programming industry fast.

Chapter 2: The Architecture of the Android Operating System

An Android operating system, regardless of version number, is composed of five software components. They are the Linux kernel, libraries, Android runtime, application framework, and applications. In case you are familiar with operating systems, Android is based on Linux, which is also based on UNIX.

As an FYI, iOS is based on OS X, which is another operating system based on UNIX. Technically, you can consider iOS and Android as cousins.

The Linux Kernel

All operating systems have a kernel. The kernel is at the bottommost layer of the Android operating system. Without it, the rest of the components of the Android operating system will be useless.

The kernel's job is to communicate and manage the devices or hardware inside a computer or smartphone. It manages the resources that are used in the device and it makes it possible for the CPU (Central Processing Unit) to communicate with other hardware components present in a device.

The kernel is capable of handling those components thanks to device drivers. A few of the usual components in an Android smartphone are the screen, camera, flash memory, keypad, Wi-Fi, speakers, and battery. All of those devices have device drivers that allow the kernel and the CPU to understand how to communicate with them.

The kernel is the core of an operating system. Without it, all the other core components in the operating system will be unusable. By the way, the Android operating system is currently using Linux 2.6 together with 115 or more patches. Due to its Linux roots, you can say that an Android device is as powerful as a computer. Heck, you can even set up an Android smartphone for use as a server in a matter of seconds.

Android Libraries

Just above the kernel are the Android libraries. In programming, libraries are reusable program components that make program development and computer operations easier. A few of the known libraries in Android are surface manager, media framework, SQLite, OpenGL, ES, FreeType, WebKit, SGL, SSL, and libc.

- SQLite: Primarily used for accessing any data published by different content providers; It has its own set of database management classes.

- SSL: This library is popular for providing internet security

- OpenGL: Provides the Java interface needed by OpenGL/ES 3D graphics for rendering API.

- Media Framework: Provides a set of media codecs to make recording and playing media of various formats possible.

- WebKit: A browser engine the facilitates the display of HTML content into applications

These libraries make things easier for programmers by preventing them from reinventing the wheel or recreating a component. For example, the WebKit is a library that contains procedures, classes, subroutines, and pre-written code to give a program the capability to browse the web.

In the case that your program will have minor browsing capabilities or it will show ad banners from the web, you can just use the functions from the WebKit library. You do not need to develop your own web browser in your program, which is an inefficient task by itself.

On the other hand, the SSL library helps programs when it comes to establishing secure internet connections, while SQLite provides database capabilities to programs. You will learn the use of the other Android libraries as you advance in your path as an Android app developer.

Android Runtime

Just beside the Android libraries in the second layer of the Android platform is Android runtime. It has two of the primary components that allow most applications on your smartphone or Android device to work. First are the core libraries. Second is the Dalvik Virtual Machine.

The two of them allow your Android devices to run programs written using Java. Primarily, the Dalvik Virtual Machine acts as a compiler for your Java applications. The Dalvik Virtual Machine reads and translates your Java programs to machine code, which allows your phone to execute them easily.

Aside from allowing Java programs to run in your phone, it also supports and performs multi threading and memory management. It means that it can allow your Java or Android programs to run simultaneously.

As an FYI, Java programs always require a virtual machine in order to run. Its primary function is to allow Java programs to run in any operating system. Normally, programs written in other languages need to be written precisely for the operating system it will run on.

Java programs, on the other hand, need to be programmed for the virtual machine. Instead of the programs being tailored for the operating systems, the virtual machine tailors itself to the operating system, which does a lot of favor to Java developers.

The Dalvik Virtual Machine was developed primarily for Android. Aside from allowing Java programs to run on mobile devices, it also makes them run optimally — in a sense that it will use less system resources and memory storage space. On the other hand, the core libraries are there to aid the Java programs to run.

Android Application Framework

The Android application framework is the third software layer in the Android operating system. It houses the much needed higher-level services and the basic functionalities of an Android device. All of the pieces of software in the Android application framework are written as Java classes, which make them dependent on the Android runtime component.

A few of the apps or services included in the Android application framework are the activity manager, window manager, content providers, view system, package manager, telephony manager, resource manager, location manager, and notification manager.

The activity manager block is often used for managing one complete activity cycle for every application. Meanwhile, the content providers block is utilized for data sharing between two different applications. The telephony manager takes care of all items related to voice calls while the location manager is in charge of all location data obtained through GPS and the cell tower. Lastly, the notifications managers enables applications to post the latest alerts; prompting the user to take action.

Android app developers need to work on these frameworks in order to make their applications seamlessly work with the Android operating system. Thankfully, Android developers can also use the framework to create much richer apps.

Android Applications

Finally, what is left is Android's application layer — the topmost one. Primarily, creating them is your goal. By default, the Android operating system comes with contacts, phone, browser, and home apps. To build an Android app, a combination of various building blocks is needed. Basic building blocks include: the activities block that handles most of the user interface acitvities as well as any inter-device interactions; the services block which takes care of the all background processing involved in the application use; broadcast receivers that are in charge of communication processes between the OS and apps; and content providers that handle any data collection or data management task.

The complexity of the app depends on how many features you include. Take note that your applications will not work in the cases where one of the other components or layers of your operating system is damaged or missing.

On the other hand, you can save a lot of time if you take advantage of the libraries and frameworks in the Android operating system. Do remember that newer versions of Android have improved frameworks and libraries. And when creating an app, be mindful of the libraries and functions that you will use.

Some functions of libraries or frameworks in newer versions of Android are not present in older versions. In case a user runs an application that requires those functions but he is using an older version of Android, the app will not work.

Chapter 3: Preparation to Android App Programming

Android application development is not easy. You must have some decent background in program development. It is a plus if you know Visual Basic and Java. And it will be definitely a great advantage if you are familiar or have already used Eclipse's IDE (Integrated Development Environment). Also, being familiar with XML will help you.

You will need a couple of things before you can start developing apps.

Your Computer

First, you will need a high-end computer. It is common that other programming development kits do not need a powerful computer in order to create applications. However, creating programs for Android is a bit different. You will need more computing power for you to run Android emulators, which are programs that can allow you to test your programs in your computer.

Using a weak computer without a decent processor and a good amount of RAM will only make it difficult for you to run those emulators. If you were able to run it, it will run slowly.

Android Device

Second, you will need an Android device. That device will be your beta tester. With it, you will know how your program will behave in an Android device. When choosing the test device, make sure that it is at par with the devices of the market you are targeting for your app. If you are targeting tablet users, use a tablet. If you are targeting smartphones, then use a smartphone.

Android SDK

Third, you will need the Android SDK (Software Development Kit) from Google. The SDK is a set of files and programs that can allow you to create and compile your program's code. As of this writing, the latest Android SDK's file size is around 350mb. It will take you 15 – 30 minutes to download it. If you uncompressed the Android SDK file, it will take up around 450mb of your computer's disk space. The link to the download page is http://developer.android.com/sdk/index.html. By the way, when you get the SDK, you will also get Android Studio.

The SDK can run on Windows XP, Windows 7, Mac OSX 10.8.5 (or higher), and Linux distros that can run 32bit applications and has glibc (GNU C library) 2.11 or higher.

Once you have unpacked the contents of the file you downloaded, open the SDK Manager. That program is the development kit's update tool. To make sure you have the latest versions of the kit's components, run the manager once in a while and download those updates. Also, you can use the SDK Manager to download older versions of SDK. You must do that in case you want to make programs with devices with dated Android operating systems.

Eclipse and ADT (Android Development Tools)

Back then, Eclipse IDE was chosen as the preferred way to develop Android apps. After all, it was the primary IDE that most Java programmers use. And since Android apps are basically Java apps for the Android operating system, people have started using Eclipse.

However, Eclipse IDE alone is not capable of making life easier for Android app developers. Due to that, ADT or Android Development Tools for Eclipse IDE was developed. ADT is a plugin for Eclipse that makes the IDE more ready in developing Android applications.

If you plan to use Eclipse, it is essential that you use the latest version of Eclipse (3.7.2 Indigo or higher). As of this writing, the latest version of Eclipse is 4.4 Luna. To get Eclipse, go to this page: http://www.eclipse.org/mobile/. Eclipse is around 200MB to 300MB big.

JRE (Java Runtime Environment) and JDK (Java Development Kit)

Any programming venture with Java involved requires the Java Runtime Environment and Java Development Kit. JRE allows a computer to run Java programs, while JDK allows a programmer to develop Java programs. Eclipse and even Android Studio, which will be discussed later, highly depend on these two.

By default, if you are using a computer running on Microsoft Windows, it is probable that you already have JRE installed. However, please do note that it is a must that your JRE is up to date. You can update your Java by just going to your computer's control panel, opening the Java control panel by clicking Java, clicking on the Update tab on the Java's control panel, and clicking the Update Now button.

On the other hand, you must download JDK as it does not come preinstalled in computers. You can download it on Oracle's website: http://www.oracle.com/technetwork/java/javase/downloads/index.html. Take note that these two programs alone can cost you 1GB to 2GB of disk space.

Android Studio

On the other hand, you have the option to use the new Android Studio. The Android Studio contains the Gradle, Google Cloud, JUnit, Maven, Live Preview, Android Studio IDE, Android SDK tools, Android 5.0 (Lollipop) platform, and Google APIs.

Most Android developers are shifting to this app development software package. As of now, it is considered the official IDE for Android apps. One of its main features is its intelligent code editor, which contains the following features: code analysis, refactoring, and advanced code/keyword completion.

Take note that just like the Android SDK, it will require a decent computer. Your computer must have 4GB RAM or more for optimal development experience. You must at least have 5GB free storage space. The installer alone requires 800MB. The Studio and Android SDK requires approximately 3GB or more. And the JDK requires 1GB. By the way, you might need to free up 2GB or more in case you need to add optional packages for your SDK.

By the way, despite being the primary development IDE for Android, you can still make do with Eclipse. Also, if you have already done any project in Eclipse, you can easily import it to Android Studio using its import function.

Installation of all those IDE is easy. Just follow the instructions. To get Android Studio, just go to the link mentioned in the Android SDK section.

Chapter 4: Basic Programming and Writing Course in Java and XML

Most of the time, you will be creating your app using the IDEs Android Studio and Eclipse. And most of the time, you will be dragging and dropping view elements, adjusting their properties, and adding some minor tweaks that can be done with a few clicks.

Unfortunately, those actions have their limits. And to be frank, you are just developing the tip of the iceberg — the app's design. Anyway, the point is that you are required to type in a few lines of code to make sure that your app will work just the way you want it.

To develop Android by manually writing source code, you must learn and get familiar with Java and XML. Java is a programming language. XML, on the other hand, is a markup language. Files written in Java end with the .java extension, while files written in XML end with the .xml extension.

Mostly, when dealing with Java in Android development, you are actually writing your program's code. Particularly, all the things that happen in your app will be dependent on your app's java code. In Android Studio, your app's main java file is located at app > src > main > java > com.example.admin.myapplication (or your app's reverse domain or package name) > MainActivity (or any name that you have assigned for your program). In case you are going to use Eclipse, the main java file should be located at src > your app's package name > app name.java.

On the other hand, you will be primarily dealing with XML if you are going to edit your app's activity and certain resources. For example, you will be editing the XML files for your activities saved in the app > src > main > res > layout. Also, you will be editing the XML file for the string values in your app in app > src > main > res > values > strings.xml.

Java Programming

Learning Java in one go can be a pain. However, you do not need to master Java in order to create a decent Android app. The important thing you should learn is how to write Java code properly by abiding to its syntax rules and familiarizing yourself with programming in general.

Syntax is a collection of rules in a language or programming languages. You can think of it as grammar rules in writing English sentences and paragraphs. Learning the syntax of a programming language is essential. Take note that one small syntax mistake in your source code's can ruin your app or make it behave the way you do not want to.

But even before you do learn the rules, you must learn the parts of the Java language. After all, learning the grammar rules in English is useless if you do not know where those rules apply — in English's case, those rules apply to the parts of the sentence.

Identifiers

Identifiers are names in programming languages. It can be used as a reference for an object, a name for a function, or a name for a variable. Identifiers make it easier for programmers to assign, invoke, and use other elements in the program.

When it comes to syntax, take note that Java is case sensitive. A variable with an identifier X is different from a variable with an identifier x.

Most Java programmers have naming conventions that they follow when creating identifiers. Writing letter case separated words (or CamelCase) is the most common naming convention for Java programmers.

When dealing with identifiers with multiple words, those words are separated with an uppercase first letter. For example: thisIsAVariable is a variable identifier that uses the letter case naming convention. By the way, it is common that the first letter of the identifier is in lower case.

Keywords

Keywords are identifiers that are reserved for special functions in a programming language. Since they are reserved, you cannot use them as identifiers for the other elements in your program. When using a source code editor or your IDE's text editor, keywords are highlighted with a different color — usually with blue — for you to easily identify them. In Java, there are around 50 keywords.

Literals

Literals are the raw data that you present to your source code. There are two common literal types that you will be using in your app's source code. The first literal type is numbers. The second type is strings. By the way, strings are text enclosed in single or double quotations. They are enclosed in quotations to prevent the compiler of Android Studio in mistaking your text as keywords, identifiers, or numbers.

Numbers can be represented in multiple ways in Java. It can be presented in decimal, octal, hexadecimal, or binary form. Other types of literals include Boolean values (truth values: true and false), null, and character.

Variables

Variables are identifiers that 'hold' data or literals. Whenever you assign literals to identifiers, they become variables. Unlike in other programming languages, you need to declare a variable and set the type of literal it can store. For example:

int thisVariableCanStoreIntegers; //This line of code declare thisVariableCanStoreIntegers as a variable that can hold integers. The line used the keyword int to tell Java that the variable's type is integer

thisVariableCanStoreIntegers = 23; //This line of code initialize the variable and assigns the integral number 23 to it

int anotherVariable = 14; //This line declares, initialize, and assign a value to the variable anotherVariable

int x, y, z; //You can declare multiple variables in one statement by using the comma (,) separator

int x = 2, y = 3, z = 4; //You can also do multiple assignments

Code Blocks

Code blocks are like paragraphs in the English language. A code block contains multiple sets of statements (or lines of codes), that work together to achieve a single goal. In some cases, the statements in code blocks are just put together to perform a batch of commands in one go.

Code blocks are used whenever you will need to create methods or classes — two things that you will learn when you advance in Java or Android app development. To contain the statements within a code block, they are enclosed inside curly braces ({}) or separators. These braces are also used to signify a new scope. For example:

```
void thisIsARandomMethod() {

    int aVariable;

    aVariable = 2;

    {
```

```
        int b;

        b = 3;

    }

}
```

In the example, a new scope was created inside the code block. Take note that anything that you do in a different scope is independent from other parent or sibling scopes. For example, the variable b cannot be used outside its scope. However, child scopes can use the variables from parent scopes. You can use the aVariable inside the child scope.

By the way, indentation in code blocks is not necessary when programming using Java. However, they do make your source code neater and cleaner.

Comments

When typing source code, there will be times that you will need to place markers, explanations, or labels in your statements. This is when comments become handy. Comments in programming languages are lines of text that are ignored by the compiler or interpreter. They actually have no use for the computer or program, but they are indispensable tools for the programmer.

It is common in source code editors that comments are highlighted in green. However, in Android Studio, comments are highlighted in gray and italicized.

When programming in Java, you have three methods or types that you can use to create comments. They are documentation comments, end of line comments, and traditional comments.

Traditional comments are created by enclosing text using the opening /* and the closing */. For example:

/* Traditional comments are commonly used

when creating comments with multiple

lines of text.

Everything inside the opening and closing

symbols are ignored by the compiler

and the computer */

Documentation comments are just like traditional comments. However, unlike the traditional comments, they are treated specially Usually, they are treated as documentation text for your source code or file. Instead of the opening /*, documentation comments start with the opening /** and close with the closing */. Also, each additional line must start with an asterisk (*). For example:

/** This is a short documentation file.

* @author: The Author of this Book

*/

Lastly, and most probably the most used kind of comment, is the end of line comment. End of line comments are placed at the end of the line and starts with //. Unlike the previous types, end of line comments do not use any closing tag. Due to that, anything written after the two slashes are considered comments. Because of that, they are usually placed at the end of a statement or a physical line. On the other hand, they can be used a standalone physical line. For example:

int dog = 3; //This comment is ignored. And will not affect the statement before it

// int cat = 4; The statement in this line will not work since it is considered a comment.

Operators and Expressions

Programming is mostly about operations and evaluation of data. In Java, multiple operators are available for to use. Some of them deal with manipulating numbers, including basic Mathematical operations. Some deals with strings. And some will provide you with program control flow.

On the other hand, take note of the term expressions. Expressions are combinations of literals, value-giving keywords or methods, operators, and variables that can be evaluated. For example:

int a = 1 + 1;

In the example, two operators were used. First is the assignment operator (=). The assignment operator allows associating a variable to a literal. Second is the addition operator (+). The addition operator adds the two numbers beside it. The expression in the statement is 1 + 1, which can be evaluated. The assignment operator will take the evaluated value of the expression to the variable.

Just like in Mathematics, operators in programming languages and Java have an order of precedence — an order which prioritizes the operators that should be evaluated first. Below is a table of most of the available operators in Java and their order of precedence.

Order of Precedence	Operator Symbol	Description / Purpose	Associativity
1	( )	Invokes methods, group	Left to Right

		variables, and literals	
	[ ]	Initialize or access an array	
	.	Selects class member or methods	
2	++ --	Increment and decrement value of the literal or variable on its left by 1 if placed to the right (postfix)	
3	++ --	Increment and decrement value of the literal or variable on its right by 1 if placed to the left (prefix)	Right to Left
	+ -	Unary minus and plus: indicates the sign of a numerical variable or literal if placed before the variable or	

		literal (prefix)	
	!	Logical NOT Negates truth values. Returns 1 if value is 0. And returns 0 if value is not 0.	
	~	Bitwise NOT negates digits in a binary literal or variable	
4	* / %	Multiplication, division, modulo (division that returns the remainder instead of the quotient)	Left to Right
5	+ -	Addition, subtraction if placed in the middle of two variables or literals	
	+	String Concatenation if placed in the middle of two	

		variables or string literals (join strings together)
6	>> << >>>	Bitwise signed right shift, left shift, unsigned right shift
7	> >=	Less than, less than or equal to (usually used for relational comparison in conditional statements)
	< <=	Greater than, Greater than or equal to (usually used for relational comparison in conditional statements)
8	== !=	Is equal to, is not equal to (usually used for relational comparison in conditional statements)
9	&	Logical and

		Bitwise AND	
10	^	Logical and Bitwise XOR	
11	|	Logical and Bitwise OR	
12	&&	Logical conditional AND	
13	||	Logical conditional OR	
14	c ? t : f	Ternary conditional ?	Right to Left
15	=	Assignment operator	
	+= -=	Add and assign, subtract and assign	
	*= /= %=	Multiply and assign, divide and assign, modulo and assign	
	<<= >>= >>>=	Bitwise left shift and assign, signed right shift and assign, unsigned right shift and	

		assign
	&= ^= |=	AND and assign, XOR and assign, OR and assign

Note that the lower the order of precedence, the higher the priority of the operator. Some operators were not included and some are not explained fully since you will not be needing them anytime soon. The operators that you will be mostly using in your apps are the mathematical, conditional, assignment, and relational/conditional operators. In some cases, you might need to use logical operators.

Statements, Physical Line, and Logical Line

A statement is composed of all or any of those parts combined. In literature, a statement is a sentence — an imperative one. Take note that it is essential that you separate the elements in your statements with spaces. It is not imperative, but usage of space in coding improves the readability of your source code.

Every statement in your source code will tell your computer or Android device to do something. A simple declaration and assignment of a variable is a statement. Statements are also called logical lines.

In Java, a statement will be considered as such if it ends with the semicolon (;) separator. Whenever you finish writing a logical line, never forget to include a semicolon. If not, you will receive a syntax error.

On the other hand, a physical line is a line of code in programming. A physical line can or cannot be a statement. As you might have noticed in source code editors, every line in the editor is numbered. A line of text or code is a physical line.

Below is an example of the initial Java code of a new app made in Android Studio:

package com.example.admin.myapplication;

import android.support.v7.app.ActionBarActivity;
import android.os.Bundle;
import android.view.Menu;
import android.view.MenuItem;

public class MainActivity **extends** ActionBarActivity {

   @Override
   protected void onCreate(Bundle savedInstanceState) {
     super.onCreate(savedInstanceState);
     setContentView(R.layout.*activity_main*);
   }

   @Override
   public boolean onCreateOptionsMenu(Menu menu) {
     // *Inflate the menu; this adds items to the action bar if it is present.*
     getMenuInflater().inflate(R.menu.*menu_main*, menu);
     return true;
   }

   @Override
   public boolean onOptionsItemSelected(MenuItem item) {
     // *Handle action bar item clicks here. The action bar will*
     // *automatically handle clicks on the Home/Up button, so long*
     // *as you specify a parent activity in AndroidManifest.xml.*
     int id = item.getItemId();

     //*noinspection SimplifiableIfStatement*

```
if (id == R.id.action_settings) {
    return true;
}

return super.onOptionsItemSelected(item);
    }
}
```

XML Writing

Primarily, you will not be writing too much XML in your app if you are going to use IDEs. After all, most of the XML writing tasks you will do should be dedicated in designing your app's appearance. Since the IDEs will do the writing for you when you drag and drop the views that you want to appear, XML writing should not be a big issue.

Nevertheless, if you want full control of your app's properties and appearance, then it is essential that you edit your app's XML files on your source code editor. Do not worry; compared to Java programming, XML writing is much easier.

If you are familiar with HTML (HyperText Markup Language), then it will be easy for you to understand XML (eXtensible Markup Language). XML is technically similar to HTML. The main difference is that XML is much simpler and straight to the point. Machines and humans (those who are familiar with XML of course) can easily understand it.

Below is an example of an activity's XML file:

```
<RelativeLayout
xmlns:android="http://schemas.android.com/apk/res/android"
   xmlns:tools="http://schemas.android.com/tools"
android:layout_width="match_parent"
   android:layout_height="match_parent"
```

```
android:paddingLeft="@dimen/activity_horizontal_margin"
  android:paddingRight="@dimen/activity_horizontal_margin"
  android:paddingTop="@dimen/activity_vertical_margin"
  android:paddingBottom="@dimen/activity_vertical_margin"
tools:context=".MainActivity">

  <TextView android:text="@string/hello_world"
android:layout_width="wrap_content"
    android:layout_height="wrap_content" />

</RelativeLayout>
```

Content and Markup

Content is the information that users will see once the XML file is processed. In Android, that's the activity screen and the elements you add to it. On the other hand, markups are words, keywords, and syntax that allow you to define content and let the machines know what to do with your content.

Elements, Opening, Closing, and Empty Element Tags

Tags are element names enclosed in chevrons (< > or less than and greater than signs). XML elements or tags depend on the machine that will read it. For example, XML files for Android apps cannot be processed the same way by other machines not running on Android. But it does not mean that it cannot be read. For example, other machines have no use or have no idea on how to process the TextView element.

A markup line always starts with an opening tag and ends with a closing tag. For example, in an activity in an Android app with a relative layout, the markup starts with <RelativeLayout> and ends with a </RelativeLayout>. Take note that the closing tag of an opening tag has the same tag with an additional slash (/) prefix.

By the way, having markup tags that require closing tags means that you can nest another markup construct inside. For example, the RelativeLayout tag is a ViewGroup that can act as a container for other View elements such as TextView (text field).

On the other hand, empty element markup tags cannot contain or nest another markup construct within it. Most empty elements in Android are View elements.

Attribute

An element in an XML file can contain attributes or properties. For example, a TextView element has an attribute or property of android:text. The attribute android:text holds the string or text that will be displayed on the screen or activity. Attributes are placed together with the opening tag that is enclosed in chevrons.

Usually, IDEs will auto populate an element's attributes once it is placed on the Design view, which makes things a whole lot easier.

By the way, Android View elements and other elements in an Android app have multitudes of attributes. Most of the time, the IDE will not put all the attributes in the XML file — unless the default values of those attributes are changed. Also, you can edit the attributes of an element by using the properties box or window in Eclipse or Android Studio.

Chapter 5: Android's Application Components

Every Android app needs four necessary components in order to be rich and decent. The components are attached in the AndroidManifest.xml — the app's manifest file. The manifest file indicates how the components interact and how they are related. The four components are:

- Services: this component manages the processes in the background created by the app.

- Activities: this component is responsible for the display and UI (User Interface). It also is responsible for the actions that the user will perform within the app's UI.

- Content Providers: this component manages data management and related issues.

- Broadcast Receivers: this component manages the communication between the app and the operating system — mainly with Android's framework.

Services

The service component is a background office. Users are mainly unaware of services. They are pushed to the background since users do not need to know or see what happens when a service is running.

Usually, services handle boring and tedious operations needed for the app to do its thing or tasks. A good example is Facebook's Messenger app. Even if you switch to another app, its services will still run. One of its services is to fetch messages from the server in case that somebody messages you in Facebook.

When creating a service in your app, you will need to put it under the Service class as a subclass. For example:

```
public class ExampleService extends Service {
    <Insert the code here for ExampleService>
}
```

Activities

You can imagine an activity as a page of your app. In simple terms, an activity is a screen UI in your app. Every activity is loaded with UI elements in order for your user to complete a task or use the app. In Facebook's Messenger app, you can access multiple activities or pages.

For example, at the start of the Messenger app, you will see a login page. When you are logged in, the app will show the activity for your friends list. When you try to message a friend in the messenger, you will be transferred to the chat activity or page.

An activity represents a single screen with a user interface. For example, an email application might have one activity that shows a list of new emails, another activity to compose an email, and another activity for reading emails. If an application has more than one activity, then one of them should be marked as the activity that is presented when the application is launched.

When creating an activity in your app, you will need to put it under the Activity class as a subclass. For example:

```
public class MainPage extends Activity {
    <Insert the code here for MainPage>

}
```

Content Providers

This component manages the flow of data from the application itself to others. The content provider can either store the data or information it has on the storage or file system, or put it in a database. Mostly, you will be using ContentResolver class methods when creating a content provider class.

When creating a content provider in your app, you will need to put it under the ContentProvider class as a subclass. For example:

public class ExampleContentProvider **extends** ContentProvider {
   <Insert the code here **for** ExampleContentProvider >

}

Broadcast Receivers

Broadcast receivers handle the messages that the system or other applications send or broadcast. Usually, broadcasts from other apps and the system tell applications about certain events such as a finished download. The broadcast receiver analyzes the message and performs the necessary action or response to the message.

When creating an activity in your app, you will need to put it under the BroadcastReceiver class as a subclass. The messages it receive are treated as Intent objects. For example:

public class ExampleBroadcastReceiver **extends** BroadcastReceiver {
   <Insert the code here **for** ExampleBroadcastReceiver>

}

Other Components

Of course, those are not the only components that your app may have. Some other components serve as 'connectors' and 'enhancements' to those. Using them wisely can get your app feature-rich and highly functional.

- Views: are the regular UI elements you typically see on activities such as lists, buttons, textboxes and etcetera.

- Fragments: unlike the views or UI elements, fragments are certain behaviors or responses on activities.

- Intents: their main function is to wire components together using messages.

- Layouts: handles and formats the appearance of views. These also manage the screen.

- Manifest: this is like the configuration or settings file of your application.

- ***Resources: are external data or files that are not coded within your application***.

Chapter 6: Starting Your First Project Using Eclipse and Android SDK

To start creating programs, you will need to open Eclipse. The Eclipse application file can be found under the eclipse folder on the extracted files from the Android SDK. Whenever you run Eclipse, it will ask you where you want your Eclipse workspace will be stored. You can just use the default location and just toggle the "don't show" checkbox.

New Project

To start a new Android application project, just click on the dropdown button of the "New" button on Eclipse's toolbar. A context menu will appear; click on the Android application project.

The New Android Application project details window will appear. In there, you will need to input some information for your project. You must provide your program's application name, project name, and package name. Also, you can configure the minimum and target SDK where your program can run and the SDK that will be used to compile your code. And lastly, you can indicate the default theme that your program will use.

Application Name

The application name will be the name that will be displayed on the Google's Play Store when you post it there. The project name will be more of a file name for Eclipse. It will be the project's identifier. It should be unique for every project that you build in Eclipse. By default, Eclipse will generate a project and package name for your project when you type something in the Application Name text box.

Package Name

The package name is not usually displayed for users. Take note that in case you develop a large program, you must remember that your package name should never be changed. On the other hand, it is common that package names are the reverse of your domain name plus your project's name. For example, if your website's domain name is www.mywebsite.com and your project's name is Hello World, a good package name for your project will be com.mywebsite.helloworld.

The package name should follow the Java package name convention. The naming convention is there to prevent users from having similar names, which could result to numerous conflicts. Some of the rules you need to follow for the package name are:

. Your package name should be all in lower caps. Though Eclipse will accept a package name with a capital letter, it is still best to adhere to standard practice.

. The reverse domain naming convention is included as a standard practice.

. Avoid using special characters in the package name. Instead, you can replace it with underscores.

. Also, you should never use or include the default com.example in your package name. Google Play will not accept an app with a package name like that.

Minimum SDK

Minimum required SDK could be set to lower or the lowest version of Android. Anything between the latest and the set minimum required version can run your program. Setting it to the lowest, which is API 1 or Android 1.0, can make your target audience wider.

Setting it to Android 2.2 (Froyo) or API 8, can make your program run on almost 95% of all Android devices in the world. The drawback fn this is that the features you can include in your program will be limited. Adding new features will force your minimum required SDK to move higher since some of the new functions in Android is not available on lower versions of the API (Application Programming Interface).

Target SDK

The target SDK should be set to the version of Android that most of your target audience uses. It indicates that you have tested your program to that version. And it means that your program is fully functional if they use it on a device that runs the target Android version.

Whenever a new version of Android appears, you should also update the target SDK of your program. Of course, before you release it to the market again, make sure that you test it on an updated device.

If a device with the same version as your set target SDK runs your program, it will not do any compatibility behavior or adjust itself to run the program. By default, you should set it to the highest version to attract your potential app buyers. Setting a lower version for your target SDK would make your program old and dated. By the way, the target SDK should be always higher or equal with the minimum target SDK version.

Compile with

The compile with version should be set to the latest version of Android. This is to make sure that your program will run on almost all versions down to the minimum version you have indicated, and to take advantage of the newest features and optimization offered by the latest version of Android. By default, the Android SDK will only have one version available for this option, which is API 20 or Android 4.4 (KitKat Wear).

After setting those all up, it is time to click on the Next button. The new page in the screen will contain some options such as creating custom launcher icon and creating activity. As of now, you do not need to worry about those. Just leave the default values and check, and click the Next button once again.

Custom Launcher Icon

Since you have left the Create Custom Launcher option checked, the next page will bring you in the launcher icon customization page. In there, you will be given three options on how you would create your launcher. Those options are launcher icons made from an image, clipart, or text.

With the text and clipart method, you can easily create an icon you want without thinking about the size and quality of the launcher icon. With those two, you can just get a preset image from the SDK or Android to use as a launcher icon. The same goes with the text method since all you need is to type the letters you want to appear on the icon and the SDK will generate an icon based on that.

The launcher icon editor also allows you to change the background and foreground color of your icon. Also, you can scale the text and clipart by changing the value of the additional padding of the icon. And finally, you can add simple 3D shapes on your icon to make it appear more professional.

Bitmap Iconography Tips

When it comes to images, you need to take note of a few reminders. First, always make sure that you will use vector images. Unlike the typical bitmap images (pictures taken from cameras or images created using Paint), vector images provide accurate and sharp images. You can scale it multiple times, but its sharpness will not disappear and will not pixelate. After all, vector images do not contain information about pixels. It only has numbers and location of the colors and lines that will appear in it. When it is scaled, it does not perform antialiasing or stretching since its image will be mathematically rendered.

In case that you will be the one creating or designing the image that you will use for your program and you will be creating a bitmap image, make sure that you start with a large image. A large image is easier to create and design.

Also, since in Android, multiple sizes of your icon will be needed, a large icon can make it easier for you to make smaller ones. Take note that if you scale a big picture into a small one, some details will be lost, but it will be easier to edit and fix and it will still look crisp. On the other hand, if you scale a small image into a big one, it will pixelate and insert details that you do not intend to show such as jagged and blurred edges.

Nevertheless, even when scaling down a big image into a smaller one, do not forget to rework the image. Remember that a poor-looking icon makes people think that the app you are selling is low-quality. And again, if you do not want to go through all that, create a vector image instead.

Also, when you create an image, make sure that it will be visible in any background. Aside from that, it is advisable to make it appear uniform with other Android icons. To do that, make sure that your image has a distinct silhouette that will make it look like a 3D image. The icon should appear as if you were looking above it and as if the source of light is on top of the image. The topmost part of the icon should appear lighter and the bottom part should appear darker.

Activity

Once you are done with your icon, click on the Next button. The page will now show the Activity window. It will provide you with activity templates to work on. The window has a preview box where you can see what your app will look like for every activity template. Below the selection, there is a description box that will tell you what each template does. For now, select the Blank Activity and click Next. The next page will ask you some details regarding the activity. Leave it on its default values and click Finish.

Once you do that, Eclipse will setup your new project. It might take a lot of time, especially if you are using a dated computer. The next chapter will discuss the programming interface of Eclipse.

Chapter 7: Getting Familiar with Eclipse and Contents of an Android App

When Eclipse has finished its preparation, you will be able to start doing something to your program. But hold onto your horses; explore Eclipse first before you start fiddling with anything.

Editing Area

In the middle of the screen, you will see a preview of your program. In it, you will see your program's icon beside the title of your program. Just left of it is the palette window. It contains all the elements that you can place in your program.

Both of these windows are inside Eclipse's editing area. You will be spending most of your time here, especially if you are going to edit or view something in your code or layout.

The form widgets tab will be expanded in the palette by default. There you will see the regular things you see in an Android app such as buttons, radio buttons, progress bar (the circle icon that spins when something is loading in your device or the bar the fills up when your device is loading), seek bar, and the ratings bar (the stars you see in reviews).

Aside from the form widgets, there are other elements that you can check and use. Press the horizontal tabs or buttons and examine all the elements you can possibly use in your program.

To insert a widget in your program, you can just drag the element you want to include from the palette and drop it in your program's preview. Eclipse will provide you visual markers and grid snaps for you to place the widgets you want on the exact place you want. Easy, right?

Take note, some of the widgets on the palette may require higher-level APIs or versions of Android. For example, the Grid Layout from the Layouts section of the palette requires API 14 (Android 4.0 Ice Cream Sandwich) or higher. If you add it in your program, it will ask you if you want to install it. In case you did include and install it, remember that it will not be compatible for older versions or any device running on API 13 and lower. It is advisable that you do not include any element that asks for installation. It might result into errors.

Output Area, Status Bar, and Problem Browser

On the bottom part of Eclipse, the status bar, problem browser, and output area can be found. It will contain messages regarding to the state of your project. If Eclipse found errors in your program, it will be listed there. Always check the Problems bar for any issues. Take note that you cannot run or compile your program if Eclipse finds at least one error on your project.

Navigation Pane

On the leftmost part of your screen is the navigation pane that contains the package explorer. The package explorer lets you browse all the files that are included in your project. Three of the most important files that you should know where to look for are:

- activity_main.xml: This file is your program's main page or window. And it will be the initial file that will be opened when you create a new project. In case you accidentally close it on your editor window, you can find it at: YourProjectName > res > layout > activity_main.xml.

- MainActivity.java: As of now, you will not need to touch this file. However, it is important to know where it is since later in your Android development activities, you will need to understand it and its contents. It is located at: YourProjectName > src > YourPackageName > MainActivity.java.

- AndroidManifest.xml: It contains the essential information that you have set up a while ago when you were creating your project file in Eclipse. You can edit the minimum and target SDK in there. It is located at YourProjectName > AndroidManifest.xml.

Aside from those files, you should take note of the following directories:

- src/: This is where most of your program's source files will be placed. And your main activity file is locafile is located.

- res/: Most of the resources will be placed here. The resources are placed inside the subdirectories under this folder.

- res/drawable-hdpi/: Your high density bitmap files that you might show in your app will go in here.

- res/layout/: All the pages or interface in your app will be located here – including your activity_main.xml.

- res/values/: The values you will store and use in your program will be placed in this directory in form of XML files.

In the event that you will create multiple projects, remember that the directory for those other projects aside from the one you have opened will still be available in your package explorer. Because of that, you might get confused over the files you are working on. Thankfully, Eclipse's title bar indicates the location and name of the file you are editing, which makes it easier to know what is currently active on the editing area.

Outline Box

Displays the current structure of the file you are editing. The outline panel will help you visualize the flow and design of your app. Also, it can help you find the widgets you want to edit.

Properties Box

Whenever you are editing a layout file, the properties box will appear below the outline box. With the properties box, you can edit certain characteristics of a widget. For example, if you click on the Hello World text on the preview of your main activity layout file, the contents of the properties box will be populated. In there, you can edit the properties of the text element that you have clicked. You can change the text, height, width, and even its font color.

Menu and Toolbar

The menu bar contains all the major functionalities of Eclipse. In case you do not know where the button of a certain tool is located, you can just invoke that tool's function on the menu bar. On the other hand, the tool bar houses all the major functions in Eclipse. The most notable buttons there are the New, Save, and Run.

As of now, look around Eclipse's interface. Also, do not do or change anything on the main activity file or any other file. The next chapter will discuss about how to run your program. As of now, the initial contents of your project are also valid as an android program. Do not change anything since you might produce an unexpected error. Nevertheless, if you really do want to change something, go ahead. You can just create another project for you to keep up with the next chapter.

Chapter 8: Testing Your Android App

By this time, even if you have not done anything yet to your program, you can already run and test it in your Android device or emulator. Why teach this first before the actual programming? Well, unlike typical computer program development, Android app development is a bit bothersome when it comes to testing.

First, the program that you are developing is intended for Android devices. You cannot actually run it normally in your computer without the help of an emulator. And you will actually do a lot of testing. Even with the first lines of code or changes in your program, you will surely want to test it.

Second, the Android emulator works slow. Even with good computers, the emulator that comes with the Android SDK is painstakingly sluggish. Alternatively, you can use BlueStacks. BlueStacks is a free Android emulator that works better than the SDK's emulator. It can even run games with it! However, it is buggy and does not work well (and does not even run sometimes) with every computer.

This chapter will focus on running your program into your Android device. You will need to have a USB data cable and connect your computer and Android. Also, you will need to have the right drivers for your device to work as a testing platform for the programs you will develop. Unfortunately, this is the preferred method for most beginners since running your app on Android emulators can bring a lot more trouble since it is super slow. And that might even discourage you to continue Android app development.

Why Android Emulators are Slow

Why are Android emulators slow? Computers can run virtual OSs without any problems, but why cannot the Android emulator work fine? Running virtual OSs is not something as resource-extensive anymore with today's computer standards. However, with Android, you will actually emulate an OS together with a mobile device. And nowadays, these mobile devices are as powerful as some of the dated computers back then. Regular computers will definitely have a hard time with that kind of payload from an Android emulator.

Luckily, there is a way for developers that have computers using Intel processors to ease up the burden of the Android SDK's emulator. And that is to download the Intel x86 Atom System Image and Intel x86 Atom System Image packages for the Android version they are going to use in the emulator. It can speed up the emulating process, but do expect that it may or may not be as fast as you would want it to be.

USB Debugging Mode

To run your program in an Android device, connect your Android to your computer. After that, set your Android into USB debugging mode. Depending on the version of the Android device you are using, the steps might change.

For 3.2 and older Android devices:

Go to Settings > Applications > Development

For 4.0 and newer Android devices:

Go to Settings > Developer Options

For 4.2 and newer Android devices with hidden Developer Options:

Go to Settings > About Phone. After that, tap the Build Number seven times. Go back to the previous screen. The Developer Options should be visible now.

Android Device Drivers

When USB debugging is enabled, your computer will install the right drivers for the Android device that you have. If your computer does not have the right drivers, you will not be able to run your program on your device. If that happens to you, visit this page: http://developer.android.com/tools/extras/oem-usb.html. It contains instructions on how you can install the right driver for your device and operating system.

Running an App in Your Android Device Using Eclipse

Once your device is already connected and you have the right drivers for it, you can now do a test run of your application. On your Eclipse window, click the Run button on the toolbar or in the menu bar.

If a Run As window appeared, select the Android Application option and click on the OK button. After that, a dialog box will appear. It will provide you with two options: running the program on an Android device or on an AVD (Android Virtual Device) or emulator.

If your computer properly identified your device, it will appear on the list. Click on your device's name and click OK. Eclipse will compile your Android app, install it on your device, and then run it. That is how simple it is.

Take note, there will be times that your device will appear offline on the list. In case that happens, there are two simple fixes that you can do to make it appear online again; 1. restart your device; 2. disable and enable the USB debugging function on your device.

Now, you can start placing widgets on your main activity file. However, always make sure that you do not place any widgets that require higher APIs.

Chapter 9: Starting a Project in Android Studio

This chapter will provide you with a step-by-step guide on how to start creating an app using Android Studio. Technically, it would be the same process with the Android SDK.

1. Open the Android Studio program. You will be greeted with a splash screen. It might take a minute or two before the studio opens up completely. Once it loads completely, a welcome page will appear.

2. In the welcome page, you will be provided with multiple options. To create a new app, double click on the Start a New Android Project option.

3. The New Project dialog box will open. It will require some information regarding you and your project. You will need to give your project a proper name in the Application Name textbox. Next, you will need to provide the company domain. In this case, just place the package name that you want —this was discussed a few chapters ago. Lastly, provide the project location — the directory in your storage device where you will save your project. Then click on the Next button.

4. After that, you will be provided with options regarding what Android devices your program will work on. Take note that you will need to choose the version of Android that your program will work on. Do not forget that lower versions of Android have older versions of libraries. Do note that according to recent Google Play statistics, Android 4.0.3 Ice Cream Sandwich is the most dominant version on the market. Almost 90% of people who download apps from Google Play use Android Ice Cream Sandwich.

   Also, TV, Wear, and Google Glass devices require higher Android versions. Smart TV commonly runs on Android

Lollipop. And Wear requires KitKat or Lollipop (Android 4.4 and 5.0). Click on Next after you set the devices.

5. You will be redirected to the activity page. In this part, you can choose an activity template for your app. You can choose from none, blank, blank activity with fragment, full screen, Google AdMob Ads, Google Maps, Google Play Services, Login, Master/Detail Flow, Navigation Drawer, Settings, and Tabbed activity templates.

   Of course, choosing any template aside from none will make things faster for you. If you want to explore and create an activity of your own, you can just choose the blank activity — despite being blank, it will come with an action bar. Click on next if you are done choosing. In case you have chosen no activity or Add No Activity, you can just click the Finish button for you to start creating your app in the IDE.

6. On the other hand, if you chose an activity, you will be redirected to a page where you can customize the activity you've chosen. By default, you will need to provide the activity's name, layout name, title, and menu resource name. If you chose an intricate activity, however, the wizard may ask you a few more things. Once you are done filling the form, hit the Finish button.

7. Hitting the Finish button will send you back to the initial screen — the welcome page. To start building your app, open the project you created by clicking Open an existing Android Studio project button. When opening a project, you must open the project folder where you saved your file.

   Once you open a project, Android Studio will open that same project whenever you open the program. In case you want to choose another project or create a new one, you must close the current project first. You can do that by clicking File and then Close Project.

Chapter 10: Fiddling with Android Studio

After creating a project in Android Studio, Gradle will create an app for you. It might take a minute or two depending on the speed of your computer. That app will contain all the default files and settings that a normal app has. The book has already discussed most of those default files and settings previously. And just like before, that new project can be ran on your test device or emulator.

Setting Up Your Test Device

Before you start creating your apps in Android Studio, you will want to edit and customize its settings first. As of this moment, you do not need to change any fancy configurations. You just need to customize the run and debugging options of Android Studio.

To do that, click on Run on the Menu bar. A context menu will appear; click on Edit Configurations. The Run/Debug Configurations window will pop up. Expand the Defaults item on the list menu on the left. Click on the Android Application item.

In that page, you can set up the target device that will be used to run or debug your app. You have three choices. You can either set Android Studio to use the Android device connected to your computer via USB, or use the Android emulator that you have created. On the other hand, you can opt to choose a chooser dialog instead. The chooser dialog will prompt you whenever you will run or debug your app. It will give you the option to run on your Android device or Android emulator.

To be honest, once Gradle generates all the important files in your project's app, you can run it almost immediately. Open an activity in your app and press the run button. If you are connected to your Android device, Android Studio will send, install, and run the app in your device.

On the other hand, if you are going to run your app in the emulator, set your virtual devices first. You can refer to the previous chapters on how to create a virtual Android device.

Updating the SDK

The next step is to update your SDK. While your program is open, click on Tools in the Menu bar. Then click on Android and click on SDK manager. When in the SDK manager window, make sure that the Updates/New checkbox is checked. On the right side, click on the Install <x> packages button.

Once you click on Install, another window will appear. All the packages will be crossed out. You need to accept the licenses that come with them in order to install them. You can do that by clicking on the Accept License radio button. After that, all the items will be checked. Afterwards, click on the Install button. Purchasing the new packages might take a long time because they are typically large files.

Exploring Android Studio

Android Studio may overwhelm you at first. Some of its features will be relatively the same as those in Eclipse. But unlike Eclipse, Android Studio is geared towards Android app creation, so you might find some extra features. Those extra features are there to make your app development life easier.

Toolbar

Just below the Menu bar is the toolbar. It hosts shortcuts for file management, editing commands, run and debugging tools, and certain Android tools.

Tool Buttons

On the left, right, and bottom sides of Android Studio, you will see the Tool Buttons bar or Tool Window shortcuts bar. The tool buttons there will allow you to open or close tool windows such as the project, favorites, structure, captures, android, messages, todo, Maven projects, Gradle, and build variants windows.

By the default, the project tool window and messages window will be open beside the tool buttons bar.

Project Tool Window

The project tool window is much like your project's directory explorer. It will provide you with a list or directory of all the files included in your app. In the previous chapter, specifically on the Navigation pane in Eclipse, you were provided with information about certain directories in your Android app.

Since Android Studio comes with third party applications such as Gradle, you might see some unfamiliar directories such as the Gradle directory. Take note that, as of now, you should focus on your app's folder only, which is the folder named app. When tweaking your app's activities, you will be moving around app > src > main > res > layout. That is the directory where your activities' .xml files will be located.

Status Bar

The status bar is located on the bottommost part of Android Studio. It will provide you with various status messages of the program and your project.

Navigation Bar

Just below the toolbar, you will see the navigation bar. It will provide you the current location of the file opened in Android Studio. You can use the navigation bar to move around in your project folder.

Tab Bar

Below the navigation bar is the tab bar. The tab bar will allow you to switch the files you have opened in your project.

Android Studio's Workspace

In the middle of it all, you can find the workspace. Depending on the file type of the file you have opened, the elements in the workspace will change. For example, if you opened a .java file, the workspace will provide a source code editor. Opening an image file will provide you with an image viewer. You cannot perform any image editing in the image viewer. All you can do is inspect the image and use a color picker.

On the other hand, you will be provided with two modes of editing if you open an activity (an .xml from the layout folder). The first mode is Design. The second mode is Text (source code editing). You can switch modes by clicking on the tab buttons on the bottom part of the workspace.

Palette

With Design mode, you can design your app's activities by dragging and dropping from the palette window. The palette window will provide you with view elements. The elements are separated into multiple categories: Layouts, Widgets, Text Fields, Containers, Date and Time, Expert, and Custom.

Component Tree

In the component tree, you will be able to browse the view elements in your activity with ease. The component tree is similar to the outline view, window, or pane in Eclipse. The view elements will be ordered according to their structure level to make them easier to find. By just clicking the name of the view element, that element will be selected on the layout view window and on the properties window.

Context Menu

In Android Studio's context menu, you can perform multiple useful tasks with just a few clicks. By the way, the context menu is the small popup window that appears on the screen whenever you press the right mouse button.

With it, you can easily delete, cut, and copy the view elements that you want. Also, you can change the view element to a different but related view element within a few clicks. For example, if you placed an analog clock display on the activity. You can easily replace it with a digital clock by morphing it.

Another neat thing about the context menu in the workspace of Android Studio is that you can easily go to the physical line in the source code where the element was declared and open it up in the source code editor. Of course, these features are not only useable in the component tree. You can do that by clicking the Go To Declaration menu item.

Layout View Window

For beginners, most of the application development processes will be done in the Layout View window. In this window, a preview of your activity or app will be shown. Aside from seeing what it would look like on a device, you can interact with it by dragging view elements from the palette on it. Every change or addition in the Layout View will affect the source code.

You can zoom in and zoom out in the Layout view. Aside from that, you can create previews of your app in landscape mode (this is particularly useful for tablet devices). On the other hand, you can set a specific device where you will 'emulate' the display of your app. You can change it to an Android smartphone, Android Wear, or Android TV. By default, Studio Android's Layout View will be set to Nexus 4.

Aside from changing the device, you can change the theme of the phone to check if your design will adapt to any themes. You can also check previews of your app in different Android versions and different screen sizes in one go. However, do note that if your computer is not that powerful, it might take a while for the previews to render. Expect that it might take a minute or two, or Android Studio might crash on you.

Properties Window

The properties window of Android Studio is almost the same with the one in Eclipse. Whenever you highlight or select a view element, all its properties will be listed in the properties box. In there, you can manually edit or change the value of the highlighted view element. Take note that all the changes you make in the properties box will update the source code of your app.

Source Code / XML Editor

When you switch to text mode, the source code / XML editor of Android Studio will replace the palette, component tree, and properties windows. You will be left with the Layout view and the source code editor itself.

Even if the Layout View is present in text mode, you cannot drag and drop elements on the preview. In case that you double click any of the elements in the Layout View window, your workspace will revert to Design mode. Also, take note that any changes that you make in the source code will update the preview in the Layout View. If you remove a view element block in the source code, it will disappear from the Layout View window immediately.

Chapter 11: Designing Your First App in Android Studio

Currently, your app does not have anything on it except for the default TextView widget/object that contains the text, "Hello World!" Now, you will be taught how to add some elements on your main activity. But before that, you should know more details about View and Viewgroup objects.

View, as mentioned a while ago, is a typical element in an Android app. Most developers and users call them as widgets. Some of the View elements that you can add on your app are text fields, buttons, sliders, and etcetera.

On the other hand, Viewgroups are containers for View elements. They serve as the parent or root for View elements or as child for other Viewgroup objects. Keep in mind that View elements are stuck with being a child of a Viewgroup object.

Viewgroups house or group View objects together. Viewgroups make it easier to handle and organize the View elements in your activities. They are invisible to the users.

A Viewgroup can contain View objects such as text fields, buttons, and even another Viewgroup object. If you are familiar with HTML, Viewgroups are like div elements. They are invisible, but they do hold other elements within them.

Go and check your project's component tree. As you can see, under Device Screen, you will see two other items. The first one is RelativeLayout. The second one is TextView. The RelativeLayout is a Viewgroup. And inside that Viewgroup is TextView, which is a View object.

In the Layout View window, you can see the TextView object that says, "Hello World!" On the other hand, you will not see any element other than that. When you click on the TextView item on the Component Tree, the Hello World text will be highlighted. But if you click on RelativeLayout, nothing will happen except for the deselection of any selected View element on the preview screen.

You can add any widget that you want for your app. When you add a view element, make sure that you check the changes on your activity's xml file. Familiarize yourself with the attributes and the name of the elements when they are placed in an activity.

By the way, whenever you place a widget on the Design view, you might have noticed that there are some green lines and arrows in the widgets. Those are guiding lines. Those lines will help you set the location of your widgets relative to the other elements on your app's screen.

On the other hand, there are other layout modes available in Android. Each view has different behaviors and can affect the way Android places the elements that you place in the layout.

Anyway, you can run and test that app. As long as you did not change anything else, the app can be opened on your device or with an Android emulator.

Part II: Familiarity with the Android System

Chapter 1: Basic Program Structure

The Android application structure is quite rigid. In order for the elements to function properly, you have to put the files in their respective places. In this chapter, we will discuss the packages in Java, which are essentially folders where you can store your classes. We will also discuss the structure of an Android project as well as how to design a navigation system.

Java Packages

When you use packages in Java, you are able to write codes that are well-organized. Your related classes become well-structured and their specific purposes are defined. What does this mean exactly? Well, you may think that packages in Java are unfamiliar; but in reality, you have most likely already used them before.

You see, it is nearly impossible to create an application that does not use classes in various packages. For instance, Java outlines a high level package called Java. Inside this package, you can find other packages like lang. This package, in turn, contains the core classes such as util and String, which contain classes such as ArrayList.

Likewise, the Android API offers a high level Android package that holds packages such as graphics, widget, and view. If you want to use the ArrayList class for your code, you should use its entire path, which is java.util.ArrayList. Do not worry though. With Java, you do not need to type so many codes or words.

Java is actually preferred by a lot of programmers because there is not much typing involved. To write a program in Java, you just have to provide the import statement. For instance, you should write import java.util.ArrayList. By writing ArrayList, you are already referring to the class in the java.util package.

Java is also preferred by a lot of programmers because they can use a similar name on multiple classes as long as these classes are placed in dissimilar packages. Keep in mind that it is very important to use different names for different classes if you plan to put them in the same package. Otherwise, an overlap may occur.

When this happens, you can get very confused and some of your data might get lost. Also, you may have a problem if you write a code that makes use of a third-party library. You need to use different names because there is a high chance that these libraries have classes that have the same names.

How Does Android Use Packages

When it comes to Android, packages are used to arrange application codes as well as manage such applications. This operating system requires that each installed application contains a package identifier which is two levels deep or higher. Let us say that you have a package and you want to name it myniceapp. Well, this name is not appropriate and will not be recognized by the system.

So instead, you need to rename it to mycompany.myniceapp. Now, this name is more appropriate and acceptable. The primary package that stores the code of your application is meant to inimitably identify your application on your device. It is also meant to allow applications to communicate and exchange vital information.

Many Java developers actually create package structures with the reverse domain scheme utilized as basis. For instance, if you are an application developer who works at a certain company and you have an official website, you should use the appropriate codes and subpackages. Let us say that your company is called GreatSoftware and your official website is located at greatsoftware.com.

All the codes of your applications should be stored in the subpackages of com.greatsoftware. If you are creating an app called SmartApp, you should store all its code at com.greatsoftware.smartapp. You can also use the subpackages under it so you can break up your code further. You can do this by splitting the model and the view code and putting them in different packages.

The File Structure of an Android Project

Android projects made using Eclipse usually have a pre-made structure with codes and resources organized into numerous folders.

- Src/ - As mentioned, this contains the source code which is created for your applications.

- Gen/ - This contains the source code which the development tools of your application autogenerate. It is not a good idea to modify the source files contained in this folder. If you do, the changes you made will only be written over the ensuing time you create a project.

- Libs/ - This contains third-party libraries that have been pre-compiled. These JAR archives can be used for your application. For instance, if you are creating an application that obtains data from social networking feeds, you should use a social networking library that another programmer has already made for you. You should put this in the libs/ folder.

- Res/ - This contains folders that contain resources for the application. These include icons, GUI layouts, menus, etc.

- Assets/ contains media that might interest you for your application. Such media include audio files, video files, and image files that are not directly used in GUI layouts.

Application Resources

As stated earlier, the res folder contains a number of resources that you may need for your application. Such resources are kept in folders inside your res folders, depending on the resource type.

Menu/ - This stores XML files that define menus which are related to the screens in the application. You can make your application show up if you click the Menu button on your device.

Drawable-*dpi/ This contains images that are used in different parts of your application. These images include launch screen icons and images that are attached to the menus or buttons.

Your projects can have numerous drawable folders with names that are based from the resolution of your device. For instance, drawable-ldpi can contain images that are used on devices with low resolution. Drawable-hdpi can contain images that are used on devices with high resolution. And the list goes on. Through this, you can come up with images that are specifically designed for a variety of screens with different sizes. These images will look clear and crisp on these screens. They will not have any blurring or scaling.

Then again, if there was not any exact resolution, your Android operating system will search for the nearest match and then either gauge it up or down so it could fit. Because of this, you can simply put all your images in the drawable-hdpi and no longer worry about different sizes.

Layout/ - This stores XML files that give a description of the layout of widgets on the screen of your application, such as text fields and buttons. You do not have to directly write an XML though. The Android tools available in Eclipse have a drag and drop editor you can use to lay out screens.

Values/ - This contains certain values that are used in your application. These values include style definitions and text strings. The strings.xml file can be used to contain text strings that are useful for GUI layouts, such as buttons or labels. It is alright if you do not want to do this. However, if you decided to do so, you will be delighted to know that it can make applications easier and quicker to decode into different languages since all your strings will be conveniently stored in a single location. Hence, you only have to have this sole file translated.

You should take note that there are many other resources that you can also use.

Android Device Navigation

The navigation between applications and the other features on Android mobile phones is usually consistent. It does not matter what the manufacturer or form of the device is. Google has provided a set of controls which you can use to navigate on your device.

The most recent versions of the Android operating system have a requirement that all devices should have Back and Home buttons to support navigation among applications and screens. Older devices that run older Android versions usually have additional buttons, such as Search and Menu.

The most recent operating system menus have even been replaced by thinner toolbars and action bars. Such toolbars are visible all the time and cannot be hidden unless you requested so. On the other hand, backwards compatibility lets you use the menus of the older version in newer applications. It also allows you to upgrade your applications so you can use the new action bars. Actually, your emulator can still provide you with a Menu button in case you wanted to run legacy applications.

Designing Effective Navigation

When it comes to developing and designing an Android application, one of the most important steps that you need to do is to identify how users would use the application. Once you find out what types of data they are most likely to interact with in the application, you have to design the interactions that let users navigate into, back, and across a variety of content within the application.

Chapter 2: Application Navigation

Navigation with Up and Back

As an Android application developer, you need to make sure that the users are able to navigate consistently. Always remember that users tend to be frustrated with certain things, such as inconsistent basic navigation. Android 3.0 has made notable changes in the area of global navigation. Android 2.3 and older versions relied on the Back button for navigation support within the application.

Back vs. Up

The Up button is mainly used to navigate an application based on hierarchical relations between screens. Let us say that screen A shows a list of certain items. When you choose an item, screen B shows up and provides more detailed information about the item that you chose. Screen B also shows an Up button that you can click to go back to screen A. You should take note that if the screen is at the topmost portion of the application, it should not have an Up button.

On the other hand, the Back button is used to navigate an application in reverse order. It is primarily based on temporal relations between the screens, instead of the hierarchy of the application. If your previously viewed screen is a hierarchical parent of your current screen, you can press the Back button to achieve the same result as when you press the Up button. Unlike the Up button, however, the Back button does not ensure that the user stays within the application although it allows him to go back to the Home screen.

The Back button also allows the user to move on to a different application. In addition, it supports certain behaviors that are not directly connected to screen-to-screen navigation. It dismisses popups, dialogs, and other floating windows, as well as contextual action bars. It also removes the highlight of selected items and hides the IME or the onscreen keyboard.

Navigation within the Application

How to Navigate to Screens with Several Entry Points

There are instances in which a screen does not have a strict position within the hierarchy of the application and it can be reached from several entry points. For instance, you can reach a settings screen from a certain screen in your application. If you press the Up button, you should be able to go back to the referring screen. It should work just like the Back button.

How to Switch Views within a Screen

When you change the view options for your screen, the functionalities of your Up and Back buttons will not be affected. Your screen will remain in the same location within the hierarchy of your application and there would not be any new navigation history created.

You can change the view by using the left or right swipes, tabs, and collapsed tabs such as the dropdown. You can also change the view by sorting or filtering a list or changing the display characteristics, such as zooming in and zooming out.

How to Navigate Between Sibling Screens

If your application supports navigation from items so it can provide a more detailed view of these items, it is usually ideal to support direction navigation from such item to another one that either follows or precedes it. For instance, in Gmail, it is easy to swipe to the right or to the left from your conversation to read an older or newer one in your inbox. Likewise, when you change view within a screen, the navigation does not change the functionality of the Back button or the Up button.

Then again, one significant exception occurs when checking out detail views that are not connected by the referring list. For instance, when you browse in the Play Store and check out applications created by the same developer, you are able to add data in your history list when you follow their links. Likewise, you are able to create history when you click on different albums made by the same artist. The Back button is able to go through every previously viewed screen.

The Up button continues to bypass such screens and move onto the most recently viewed screen. Actually, you can improve the functionality of the Up button if you are knowledgeable on detail views. For instance, you can extend the Play Store and visualize its user to navigate from a Book option to a Movie adaption of the Book option. In this case, he can use the Up button so he can go to Movies, which he has not checked out before.

How to Navigate Into Your Application Using Home Screen Widgets and Notifications

If you wish to directly navigate to screens within the hierarchy of your application, you can use Home screen notifications or widgets. For instance, you can use the widget of Gmail Inbox as well as new message notifications so you can view conversations directly. Both of these widgets have the ability to bypass your Inbox screen.

So how should you use the Up button in these cases? Well, if your destination screen can be reached from a certain screen within your application, you should use the Up button to navigate to that screen. Otherwise, you should use the Up button to go Home or the topmost portion of your application.

As for the Back button, you can have a more predictable navigation by inserting the upward navigation path into the back stack of the task. This upward navigation path is directed to the topmost portion of the screen of the application. This lets the user remember how he entered your application to navigate to the topmost portion of the screen before he exited. For instance, in Gmail, the home screen widget features a button for directly diving to the compose screen. Either the Up or the Back buttons from this screen can take users to the Inbox. From there, they can use the Back button to go back to Home.

Indirect Notifications

If your application needs to show information regarding multiple events simultaneously, you can program it to use a notification that directs users to the interstitial screen. Such screen summarizes these events as well as provides a path that they can use to dive deeper into the application. The notifications that direct users to such screen are known as indirect notifications.

However, unlike with standard notifications, you will be redirected to the point wherein the notification was activated from when you press the Back button from the interstitial screen of an indirect notification. There would not be any extra screens inserted into your back stack. When the users proceed into the application from their interstitial screen, the Up and Back buttons act like standard notifications.

They navigate within the application instead of going back to the interstitial screen. For instance, in Gmail, users receive indirect notifications from Calendar. When they touch this notification, an interstitial screen will open up. This screen displays important reminders for a variety of events. When they touch the Back button from this screen, they will be directed back to Gmail.

Conversely, if they touch a certain event, they will be taken away from this screen and brought to the full Calendar application in which more details about the event are shown. They can use the Up and the Back buttons to navigate to the topmost portion of the Calendar.

How About Popup Notifications?

Popup notifications have the ability to bypass the notification drawer. They generally show up in front of the user. However, they are not very frequently used. They are also meant to be reserved for events in which timely responses are necessary. They can also be used whenever the context of the user has to be interrupted.

For instance, Talk makes use of this style to alert users of invitations for video chat. Each time a user wants another user to video chat, a Talk notification appears. If after several seconds, the other user does not response, the notification expires automatically. When it comes to navigation, popup notifications generally follow the behaviors of the interstitial screens of indirect notifications.

The Back button gets rid of the popup notification. When the user navigates from his popup into a notifying application, the Up and the Back buttons abide by the rules of the standard notifications for navigating within the application.

Navigating Between Applications

Among the most significant strengths of the Android operating system is the ability of the applications to activate one another. Because of this, the user is able to directly navigate from a certain application to another.

For instance, if you want to take a picture, you can use the Camera application. Through this application, you can capture your desired image and wait for that image to be returned to the referring application. This can be any application, but Gallery is most commonly used to store the captured images.

This is truly great for the application developer and the user. As a developer, you can easily leverage your codes from your other applications. Your users, on the other hand, can enjoy a smooth and hassle-free experience of picture taking.

In order for you to understand application to application navigation, you need to understand the framework behavior of the Android operating system. Let us discuss the activities, intents, and tasks.

In Android, activity refers to a component of application that defines a screen of information. It also includes all the associated actions that the user can make. Your application is a collection of activities that consist of the activities that you create and the activities that you re-use from other applications.

Task refers to the activity sequence that users follow in order to achieve a goal. In fact, a single task can use different activities from a single application. It may also use activities from numerous applications.

Intent refers to the mechanism that an application uses to signal another application that it needs assistance in executing a particular action. The activities of an application indicate which intents they are allowed to respond to. Share and other common intents, for instance, may be easily executed through a variety of applications.

Sharing Between Applications

In order for you to have a better understanding on how tasks, intents, and activities work together, you should consider how a particular application lets users share their content by using another application.

For instance, when a user launches the Play Store application from his Home screen, a new task will be started. Once he navigates through the Play Store application and touches a certain item, he will remain in the same task and extend it by doing more activities.

Let us say that he takes interest in one of the endorsed books in the Play Store, he can hover and touch this option to see more details about it. After that, he has the option to either stay or leave. If he decides to share his activities, he can use the Share button. Once he triggered this action, he will be prompted with a dialog box.

This dialog box contains a list of his activities from a variety of applications, and all of these applications are allowed to handle his Share intent. If he wants to share his actions through Gmail, the compose activity of Gmail will be added to the list as a continuation of his first task. A new task will not be created. If Gmail already runs a task in the background, it will simply ignore the new task.

Chapter 3: Action Bars and Navigation Drawers

Action Bar

The action bar is located at the topmost portion of the screen of the application. Some of its primary functions include making significant actions accessible and prominent in a predictable pattern, such as Search or New; viewing switching within applications and supporting consistent navigation; reducing clutter by executing action overflow for actions that are not frequently used; and providing a special space for giving an application its identity.

If you have just started creating applications for the Android operating system, you should take note that the action bar is among the most significant design elements you can have.

The action bar is generally categorized into four functional sections. Most applications have these four sections: the application icon, view control, action buttons, and action overflow.

The application icon establishes the identity of your application. You can replace it with different brands or logos if you want. Keep in mind that if your application does not display the top level screen, you should place the Up caret to the left portion of your application icon so your users can easily navigate up the hierarchy.

The view control refers to how users can view the data in your application. For instance, if your application shows data in multiple ways, this particular section of your action bar will let your users change views. Popular examples of view switching controls include tab controls and drop down menus.

If your application does not support different views, you can use this section to show non-interactive content, such as long details about branding or the title of the application.

The action buttons display the most crucial actions of your applications. The actions that do not fit in your action bar are automatically transferred to the action overflow. If you want to view the name of your actions, you can press a certain icon for a few seconds.

The action overflow, on the other hand, moves actions that are not frequently used to the action overflow.

Adjusting to Screen Rotation and Different Sizes of Screens

When it comes to creating an application, see to it that you consider how you can adjust to screen rotation and different sizes of screens. You can adapt to these changes by making use of split action bars that will let you distribute their content across a variety of bars located below your screen or primary action bar.

What to Consider for Split Action Bars

If you wish to split up your content across different action bars, you can choose from three different locations. These are the main action bar, the top bar, and the bottom bar. If you want your users to be able to quickly switch between views, you can put a spinner or a tab in the top bar of your application. If you want to display the action overflow and the actions, you should use the bottom bar.

Action Buttons

The action buttons on the action bar of your application displays activities. Hence, you should consider which of your buttons are most often used and then organize them accordingly. The Android operating system usually displays the most important actions as action buttons and moves the others to the action overflow. Your action bar must only display actions that are available to users. If a certain action is not available, you should hide it. You should not let others see that it is disabled.m

How to Prioritize Actions

If you are having a hard time prioritizing your actions, you can use the FIT scheme. FIT actually stands for Frequent, Important, and Typical.

An action can be considered Frequent if the users use it at least seven out of ten times whenever they visit the screen. It can also be considered Frequent if such users use it a few times in a row.

An action can be considered Important if the users find this action to be cool or interesting. It can also be labeled as Important if it does not require much effort to be executed.

An action can be considered Typical if it is presented as a first-class action in other similar applications. Likewise, it can be considered Typical if users become surprised when it is buried in the action overflow.

Once you have classified your actions to be Frequent, Important, or Typical, you should place them in your action bar. Else, you should place them in the action overflow.

Action Bar

The action bar is located at the topmost portion of the screen of the application. Some of its primary functions include making significant actions accessible and prominent in a predictable pattern, such as Search or New; viewing switching within applications and supporting consistent navigation; reducing clutter by executing action overflow for actions that are not frequently used; and providing a special space for giving an application its identity.

If you have just started creating applications for the Android operating system, you should take note that the action bar is among the most significant design elements you can have.

The action bar is generally categorized into four functional sections. Most applications have these four sections: the application icon, view control, action buttons, and action overflow.

The application icon establishes the identity of your application. You can replace it with different brands or logos if you want. Keep in mind that if your application does not display the top level screen, you should place the Up caret to the left portion of your application icon so your users can easily navigate up the hierarchy.

The view control refers to how users can view the data in your application. For instance, if your application shows data in multiple ways, this particular section of your action bar will let your users change views. Popular examples of view switching controls include tab controls and drop down menus.

If your application does not support different views, you can use this section to show non-interactive content, such as long details about branding or the title of the application.

The action buttons display the most crucial actions of your applications. The actions that do not fit in your action bar are automatically transferred to the action overflow. If you want to view the name of your actions, you can press a certain icon for a few seconds.

The action overflow, on the other hand, moves actions that are not frequently used to the action overflow.

Adjusting to Screen Rotation and Different Sizes of Screens

When it comes to creating an application, see to it that you consider how you can adjust to screen rotation and different sizes of screens. You can adapt to these changes by making use of split action bars that will let you distribute their content across a variety of bars located below your screen or primary action bar.

What to Consider for Split Action Bars

If you wish to split up your content across different action bars, you can choose from three different locations. These are the main action bar, the top bar, and the bottom bar. If you want your users to be able to quickly switch between views, you can put a spinner or a tab in the top bar of your application. If you want to display the action overflow and the actions, you should use the bottom bar.

Action Buttons

The action buttons on the action bar of your application displays activities. Hence, you should consider which of your buttons are most often used and then organize them accordingly. The Android operating system usually displays the most important actions as action buttons and moves the others to the action overflow. Your action bar must only display actions that are available to users. If a certain action is not available, you should hide it. You should not let others see that it is disabled.

How to Prioritize Actions

If you are having a hard time prioritizing your actions, you can use the FIT scheme. FIT actually stands for Frequent, Important, and Typical.

An action can be considered Frequent if the users use it at least seven out of ten times whenever they visit the screen. It can also be considered Frequent if such users use it a few times in a row.

An action can be considered Important if the users find this action to be cool or interesting. It can also be labeled as Important if it does not require much effort to be executed.

An action can be considered Typical if it is presented as a first-class action in other similar applications. Likewise, it can be considered Typical if users become surprised when it is buried in the action overflow.

Once you have classified your actions to be Frequent, Important, or Typical, you should place them in your action bar. Else, you should place them in the action overflow.

Navigation Drawer

The navigation drawer is basically a panel that shows up at the left portion of the screen to display the primary navigation options of the application. Your user can make the navigation drawer appear either by swiping from the left side of the screen towards the right or by pressing the icon of the application on the action bar.

When the navigation drawer expands, the content is showed. When it is extended fully, the action bar adjusts accordingly so that its contents are shown. It does this by replacing the existing action bar title with the name of the application and getting rid of any contextual actions that run in the background. As for the overflow menu for Help and Settings, it stays visible.

The drawer panel can be opened by pressing the navigator drawer indicator. Navigation drawers are transparent, which is why they make views more organized. They can even be used at deeper navigation hierarchy levels. Users can switch to the important screens in their application from anywhere in such application. If they decided that they want to dismiss the navigation drawer, they can simply touch the content outside it.

They can also swipe to the left side of their screen, touch the icon or title of the application in the action bar, or press the Back button. Then again, you should take note that the navigation drawer must not be used as a general replacement for the top level navigation. You should use the structure of your application as a guideline on how to choose patterns for top level switching.

Where Should You Use Navigation Drawers?

Well, you can use navigation drawers if you have at least three unique top level views. A navigation drawer is efficient in concurrently showing large numbers of navigation targets.

You can also use them if your application has to cross navigate from a lower level. The navigation drawer can be accessed from anywhere in your application, which is why it can navigate from lower level screens to a different location in the application.

In addition, you can use navigation drawers if you have deep navigation branches. As you know, navigating to the top level of the application can become cumbersome and repetitive.

Hence, you need to find a way to navigate upwards more efficiently and quickly. Navigation drawers are perfect for this because they can be accessed from any location in the application.

Navigation Hubs

Keep in mind that the navigation drawer reflects the structure of your application as well as shows its primary navigation hubs. Navigation hubs are where users go to most often. They are also frequently used as jumping off points to other locations in the application. The navigation hubs correspond to the major areas of the application which is why they get the top level views.

If your application has a deep structure, you can use low level screens that users are most likely to visit. These screens can also serve as navigation hubs. In order to expedite access to navigation drawers, all your screens that correspond to your navigation drawer entries must display the indicator of your navigation drawer. It should be shown near the icon of the application in your action bar.

You can touch the icon of your application to make your navigation drawer slide in from the left part of your screen. All of the other low level screens should display the Up button near the icon of your application. You should still be able to access the navigation drawer when you swipe your finger across the screen, although it should not show up in your action bar.

Navigation Drawer Content

It is important for you to keep the contents of your navigation drawer focused on your application navigation. You should expose your navigation hubs as list items. There should be one item for every row.

You can organize your navigation targets by including titles. There is no need for you to make them interactive. You simply have to organize your navigation targets into topics that are functional. In case you have a lot of navigation targets, you can use titles to guide your users within the navigation drawer.

Your navigation targets may have leading icons and training counters. These elements are optional, however. So it is alright if you do not use them. Nonetheless, you should use your navigation counters to tell users whenever a state of data has been changed in a certain view.

What if you have a lot of views with subordinates? If this is the case, you can collapse them into a single expandable item. This will allow you to save space. Your navigation drawer parent will turn into a split item and its left side will allow users to navigate to the view of the parent item. The right side, on the other hand, will expand or collapse the list of its child items.

It is up to your discretion how you want the initial state of your collapsible items to be. Then again, there is a general rule that the top level view entries of navigation drawers have to be visible. So if you have a lot of collapsible items, you may want to collapse every item to let your users see the entire top level views.

When your users expand your navigation drawers, the task focus switches to choosing an item from your navigation drawer. Since the navigation drawers do not overlay your action bar, your users may not immediately notice that the items in your action bar do not necessarily affect the navigation drawers.

In order to lessen your confusion, you have to adjust the contents of your action bar, such as the icon and the name of your application. You should also remove any action from your action bar that is contextual to your underlying view. If you wish to retain actions using global scope, you may do so.

What's more, you should adjust your overflow menu with your navigation targets like Help and Settings. It is not advisable to place your actions in your navigation drawer. Remember that actions are meant to be placed in the action bar. Your users expect to see such actions there.

Not every application uses navigation drawers though. You may feel tempted to expose all the capabilities of your application in just one location. However, you should be careful with what you do. You should only put your actions in a location where all applications show them. The same thing applies to navigation targets, including Help and Settings.

There are times wherein users see a contextual action bar or CAB in place of the action bar of the application. This usually occurs when the users choose multiple items or texts after a press and hold gesture. Even though the contextual action bar is visible, make sure that you still let the users open the navigation drawers by edge swiping.

You should replace the contextual action bar with a regular action bar while your navigation drawer stays open. If your users dismiss the navigation drawer, then now is the time for you to display your contextual action bar again.

How Can You Introduce Your Users to the Navigation Drawer?

Once you launch your application, see to it that you introduce your users to the navigation drawers by opening them immediately. When they see these navigation drawers, they will be prompted to explore the contents of your application and know more about its structure.

You should continue launching your application with your navigation drawers open until you are confident that your users completely understand how to use it. Then, you can launch your application with your navigation drawers closed.

Moreover, see to it that you let your users take a quick look at your navigation drawer each time their fingers make contact with the screen. This will allow them to discover the navigation drawer as well as encourage them to provide feedback.

If you open your navigation drawer from a screen represented inside it, you should highlight such entry inside the navigation drawer. Likewise, if you open your navigation drawer from a screen not listed in it, you should not highlight any of the items inside the navigation drawer.

How Does a Navigation Drawer Impact the Overall Navigation of an Application?

You should take note that the navigation drawer is practically a substitute to other top level navigation patterns. If you want your applications with navigation drawers to consistently work with applications that use spinner patterns or tabs, you should consider several important factors.

For instance, keep in mind that touching the System Back at the top portion of your application does not open the navigation drawer. The System Back only functions according to the rules of navigation for the top level, such as navigating towards the Home screen or towards a previous application within the task.

You should also remember that when your users navigate to a lower hierarchy screen from your navigation drawer with such screen having a direct parent, the Back stack option resets and the Back option points to the parent of the target screen. The same Back behavior can be observed when users navigate into applications from a notification.

Finally, you should take note that the width of your navigation drawer essentially depends on the contents that you want to show. However, such contents should only be between 240 dp and 320 dp. You should not use line items that have a height falling below 48 dp. See to it that you also choose a navigation drawer background that best matches the theme of your application.

Chapter 4: Applications with User Information and Location

User Information

The Contacts Provider is basically the central repository of the contact information of the user. This includes data from social networking and contacts applications. In such applications, you can find Contacts Provider either by sending intents to a contacts application or calling ContentResolver.

How to Retrieve a Contact List

If you want to create an application that displays the information and location of the user, you should know how to retrieve lists of contacts with data that partly or completely match a search string. You can use a variety of techniques for this.

When matching contact names, you should get a list of contacts. You can do this by matching the search string with all or part of your contact name data. In order to return a list of matches, you should use the Contacts Provider. It allows for multiple instances of a similar name.

When matching a particular data type, such as phone numbers, you should get a list of contacts as well. You can do this by matching the search string with a certain type of data, such as e-mail addresses. Through this technique, you can list every one of your contacts who have an e-mail address that matches your search string.

When matching any type of data, you should once again get a list of contacts. You can do this matching your search string to any detail data, such as names, phone numbers, street addresses, and e-mail addresses among others. This technique will enable you to accept all types of data for a search string and list all the contacts that match it.

How to Retrieve Contact Details

It is not unusual for Android users to want to retrieve contact details, including phone numbers and e-mail addresses. As an application developer, you can either provide them with all the contact details or just show the details of a certain type of data, such as e-mail address.

Anyway, if you want to retrieve all of the contact details, you can search ContactsContract.Data for rows that contain the LOOKUP KEY of the contact. You can find this column in ContactsContract.Data. You should take note that retrieving all of the contact details tends to reduce the performance of devices.

This is because doing so requires the retrieval of all the columns in ContactsContrast.Data. So before you do this procedure, see to it that you consider the performance of your Android device.

On the other hand, if you are only going to retrieve certain contact data types, you should do the same process as with retrieving all of the contact details. However, you need to make a few changes with the projection, selection, and sort order.

Using Intents to Modify Contacts

Intents are very useful when it comes to modifying contact data even though it does not directly access the Contacts Provider. It starts the contacts application, which runs the necessary Activity.

You can use an Intent to upgrade or insert a contact. This will allow you to save time and energy in developing a code and a user interface. It will also let you avoid errors that have been caused by certain modifications that do not abide by the rules of the Contacts Providers.

Furthermore, it will allow you to reduce the amount of permissions that you need to make requests. Your applications will no longer need any permission to contact the Contacts Provider.

133

Inserting a New Contact with an Intent

As an application developer, you may want to let your users insert new contacts when the application receives new data. Let us say that your Android application is designed to review restaurants. You may want your users to add restaurants as their contacts while they review them. This is such a great idea since they can contact the restaurant easily in case they want to go back.

So what should you do to make this happen? Well, you need to build the intent by using as much data as you can. Afterwards, you should send your intent to the contacts application. When you use the contacts application to insert a contact, you are also able to insert a new raw contact into the ContactsContract.RawContacts table of your Contacts Provider.

Editing Existing Contacts with an Intent

An intent is also useful in allowing users to re-write or edit their existing data. Let us say that your application can store contacts with postal addresses. If your users want to add their postal codes, you should give them the option to search for the appropriate code and add it to their data.

In order to edit existing contact data using the intent, you should use the same technique you used when inserting contact data. You should build the intent but do not forget to add the Contacts.CONTENT_LOOKUP_URI of the contact as well as its MIME type. If you wish to edit existing contact details, you can place them in the extended data of the intent. Take note that some of the name columns cannot be edited with an Intent.

Finally, you should send the intent. After this, you can expect the contacts application to display an edit screen. Once your users finish editing and saving their new contact data, the contacts application will display a contact list. Your application will be displayed when your users taps on the Back button.

Adding a Quick Contact Badge to the User Interface

QuickContactBadge is a widget that appears in the form of a thumbnail. Even though it is alright for you to use any Bitmap for your thumbnails, it is more ideal to use a Bitmap that has been decoded from the photo thumbnail of the contact. This tiny image will serve as a control whenever a user clicks on it.

Anyway, QuickContactBadge tends to expand into dialogs that contain large images and icons of applications. The large images are usually related to the contact. If there is no available image, you can use a placeholder graphic.

As for the icons of applications, they are usually handled by built-in applications. For instance, if one of a user's contacts has more than one e-mail address, an e-mail icon will show up. Once he clicks on this icon, all the e-mail addresses of his particular contact will appear. This will allow him to choose which e-mail address to contact.

User Location

Specific longitude and latitude coordinates can show the location of a user. As an application developer, it is crucial for your application to show the geographic coordinates of the location of users so they can know what street they are on or what landmark is nearby.

Location Awareness

Mobile applications typically feature the location of the user. As you know, users often take their mobile phones with them wherever they go. Hence, adding location awareness to your application will provide them with a more contextual experience. However, if you are still using Android framework location APIs, you may want to consider switching to Google Play services location APIs.

You can use Google Play services location APIs to request for the last known location of a particular device. Usually, the current location of the user is registered as the last known location of his device. Nonetheless, you can also use the fused location provider to obtain its last known location. It is among the location APIs of Google Play. It manages location technologies, provides APIs, and optimizes batter power usage.

Chapter 5: Sample Programs

Now that you've learned about the basic concepts in Android development, it's time to try out some simple programs that you also use in your own app.

I. Sample Programs for 2D Graphics

This section includes sample programs for drawing basic 2D shapes such as points, lines and circles.

1. Drawing a Single Point

```
package app.test;

import android.app.Activity;

import android.graphics.Bitmap;

import android.graphics.Canvas;

import android.graphics.Color;

import android.graphics.Paint;

import android.graphics.Path;

import android.graphics.Typeface;

import android.os.Bundle;

import android.widget.ImageView;


public class Test extends Activity {

  ImageView drawingImageView;
```

```
@Override
public void onCreate(Bundle savedInstanceState) {
  super.onCreate(savedInstanceState);
  setContentView(R.layout.main);
  drawingImageView = (ImageView)
this.findViewById(R.id.DrawingImageView);
  Bitmap bitmap = Bitmap.createBitmap((int)
getWindowManager()
    .getDefaultDisplay().getWidth(), (int)
getWindowManager()
    .getDefaultDisplay().getHeight(),
Bitmap.Config.ARGB_8888);
  Canvas canvas = new Canvas(bitmap);
  drawingImageView.setImageBitmap(bitmap);

  Paint paint = new Paint();
  paint.setColor(Color.GREEN);
  paint.setStrokeWidth(100);
  canvas.drawPoint(199, 201, paint);
  }
}
```

2. Drawing a Single Line

```
package app.test;

import android.app.Activity;

import android.graphics.Bitmap;

import android.graphics.Canvas;

import android.graphics.Color;

import android.graphics.Paint;

import android.graphics.Path;

import android.graphics.Typeface;

import android.os.Bundle;

import android.widget.ImageView;


public class Test extends Activity {

ImageView drawingImageView;


@Override

public void onCreate(Bundle savedInstanceState) {

super.onCreate(savedInstanceState);

setContentView(R.layout.main);

drawingImageView = (ImageView)
this.findViewById(R.id.DrawingImageView);

Bitmap bitmap = Bitmap.createBitmap((int)
getWindowManager()

    .getDefaultDisplay().getWidth(), (int)
getWindowManager()
```

```
    .getDefaultDisplay().getHeight(),
Bitmap.Config.ARGB_8888);
  Canvas canvas = new Canvas(bitmap);
  drawingImageView.setImageBitmap(bitmap);


  // Line
  Paint paint = new Paint();
  paint.setColor(Color.GREEN);
  paint.setStrokeWidth(10);
  int startx = 50;
  int starty = 100;
  int endx = 150;
  int endy = 210;
  canvas.drawLine(startx, starty, endx, endy, paint);
 }
}
```

3. Drawing a Circle

```
    package app.test;


    import android.app.Activity;
    import android.graphics.Bitmap;
    import android.graphics.Canvas;
```

```
import android.graphics.Color;

import android.graphics.Paint;

import android.os.Bundle;

import android.widget.ImageView;


public class Test extends Activity {

ImageView drawingImageView;


@Override

public void onCreate(Bundle savedInstanceState) {

super.onCreate(savedInstanceState);

setContentView(R.layout.main);

drawingImageView = (ImageView)
this.findViewById(R.id.DrawingImageView);

Bitmap bitmap = Bitmap.createBitmap((int)
getWindowManager()

    .getDefaultDisplay().getWidth(), (int) getWindowManager()

    .getDefaultDisplay().getHeight(),
Bitmap.Config.ARGB_8888);

Canvas canvas = new Canvas(bitmap);

drawingImageView.setImageBitmap(bitmap);


// Circle
```

```
Paint paint = new Paint();
paint.setColor(Color.GREEN);
paint.setStyle(Paint.Style.STROKE);
float x = 50;
float y = 50;
float radius = 20;
canvas.drawCircle(x, y, radius, paint);
  }
}
```

4. Drawing an Oval

```
package app.test;


import android.app.Activity;
import android.graphics.Bitmap;
import android.graphics.Canvas;
import android.graphics.Color;
import android.graphics.Paint;
import android.graphics.RectF;
import android.os.Bundle;
import android.widget.ImageView;


public class Test extends Activity {
  ImageView drawingImageView;
```

```
@Override

public void onCreate(Bundle savedInstanceState) {

  super.onCreate(savedInstanceState);

  setContentView(R.layout.main);

  drawingImageView = (ImageView)
this.findViewById(R.id.DrawingImageView);

  Bitmap bitmap = Bitmap.createBitmap((int)
getWindowManager()

      .getDefaultDisplay().getWidth(), (int) getWindowManager()

      .getDefaultDisplay().getHeight(),
Bitmap.Config.ARGB_8888);

  Canvas canvas = new Canvas(bitmap);

  drawingImageView.setImageBitmap(bitmap);


  // Oval

  Paint paint = new Paint();

  paint.setColor(Color.GREEN);

  paint.setStyle(Paint.Style.STROKE);

  float leftx = 20;

  float topy = 20;

  float rightx = 50;

  float bottomy = 100;

  RectF ovalBounds = new RectF(leftx, topy, rightx, bottomy);
```

```
canvas.drawOval(ovalBounds, paint);
}
```

5. Drawing a Polygon

```
/*
* Copyright (C) 2007 The Android Open Source Project
*
* Licensed under the Apache License, Version 2.0 (the "License");
* you may not use this file except in compliance with the License.
* You may obtain a copy of the License at
*
*     http://www.apache.org/licenses/LICENSE-2.0
*
* Unless required by applicable law or agreed to in writing, software
* distributed under the License is distributed on an "AS IS" BASIS,
* WITHOUT WARRANTIES OR CONDITIONS OF ANY KIND, either express or implied.
* See the License for the specific language governing permissions and
* limitations under the License.
*/
```

```
package app.test;

import android.app.Activity;
import android.content.Context;
import android.graphics.Canvas;
import android.graphics.Color;
import android.graphics.Matrix;
import android.graphics.Paint;
import android.graphics.Picture;
import android.graphics.Rect;
import android.graphics.RectF;
import android.graphics.drawable.Drawable;
import android.os.Bundle;
import android.util.AttributeSet;
import android.view.View;
import android.view.ViewGroup;
import android.view.ViewParent;

public class Test extends GraphicsActivity {

    @Override
    protected void onCreate(Bundle savedInstanceState) {
        super.onCreate(savedInstanceState);
```

```
    setContentView(new SampleView(this));
}
  private static class SampleView extends View {
    private Paint  mPaint = new
Paint(Paint.ANTI_ALIAS_FLAG);
    private Matrix  mMatrix = new Matrix();
    private Paint.FontMetrics mFontMetrics;

    private void doDraw(Canvas canvas, float src[], float dst[]) {
      canvas.save();
      mMatrix.setPolyToPoly(src, 0, dst, 0, src.length >> 1);
      canvas.concat(mMatrix);

      mPaint.setColor(Color.GRAY);
      mPaint.setStyle(Paint.Style.STROKE);
      canvas.drawRect(0, 0, 64, 64, mPaint);
      canvas.drawLine(0, 0, 64, 64, mPaint);
      canvas.drawLine(0, 64, 64, 0, mPaint);

      mPaint.setColor(Color.RED);
      mPaint.setStyle(Paint.Style.FILL);
      // how to draw the text center on our square
      // centering in X is easy... use alignment (and X at
midpoint)
```

```
float x = 64/2;

// centering in Y, we need to measure ascent/descent first

float y = 64/2 - (mFontMetrics.ascent +
mFontMetrics.descent)/2;

canvas.drawText(src.length/2 + "", x, y, mPaint);

canvas.restore();

}

public SampleView(Context context) {

super(context);

// for when the style is STROKE

mPaint.setStrokeWidth(4);

// for when we draw text

mPaint.setTextSize(40);

mPaint.setTextAlign(Paint.Align.CENTER);

mFontMetrics = mPaint.getFontMetrics();

}

@Override

protected void onDraw(Canvas canvas) {

canvas.drawColor(Color.WHITE);


canvas.save();

canvas.translate(10, 10);

// translate (1 point)
```

```
doDraw(canvas, new float[] { 0, 0 }, new float[] { 5, 5 });
canvas.restore();


canvas.save();
canvas.translate(160, 10);
// rotate/uniform-scale (2 points)
doDraw(canvas, new float[] { 32, 32, 64, 32 },
        new float[] { 32, 32, 64, 48 });
canvas.restore();


canvas.save();
canvas.translate(10, 110);
// rotate/skew (3 points)
doDraw(canvas, new float[] { 0, 0, 64, 0, 0, 64 },
        new float[] { 0, 0, 96, 0, 24, 64 });
canvas.restore();


canvas.save();
canvas.translate(160, 110);
// perspective (4 points)
doDraw(canvas, new float[] { 0, 0, 64, 0, 64, 64, 0, 64 },
        new float[] { 0, 0, 96, 0, 64, 96, 0, 64 });
canvas.restore();
```

```
    }
   }
}
class GraphicsActivity extends Activity {
  // set to true to test Picture
  private static final boolean TEST_PICTURE = false;

  @Override
  protected void onCreate(Bundle savedInstanceState) {
    super.onCreate(savedInstanceState);
  }
  @Override
  public void setContentView(View view) {
    if (TEST_PICTURE) {
     ViewGroup vg = new PictureLayout(this);
     vg.addView(view);
     view = vg;
    }
    super.setContentView(view);
  }
}
class PictureLayout extends ViewGroup {
  private final Picture mPicture = new Picture();
```

```
public PictureLayout(Context context) {
  super(context);
}
public PictureLayout(Context context, AttributeSet attrs) {
  super(context, attrs);
}


@Override
public void addView(View child) {
  if (getChildCount() > 1) {
    throw new IllegalStateException(
      "PictureLayout can host only one direct child");
  }
  super.addView(child);
}
@Override
public void addView(View child, int index) {
  if (getChildCount() > 1) {
    throw new IllegalStateException(
      "PictureLayout can host only one direct child");
  }
  super.addView(child, index);
}
```

```
@Override
public void addView(View child, LayoutParams params) {
  if (getChildCount() > 1) {
    throw new IllegalStateException(
      "PictureLayout can host only one direct child");
  }
  super.addView(child, params);
}
@Override
public void addView(View child, int index, LayoutParams
params) {
  if (getChildCount() > 1) {
    throw new IllegalStateException(
      "PictureLayout can host only one direct child");
  }
  super.addView(child, index, params);
}
@Override
protected LayoutParams generateDefaultLayoutParams() {
  return new LayoutParams(LayoutParams.MATCH_PARENT,
    LayoutParams.MATCH_PARENT);
}
@Override
```

```
protected void onMeasure(int widthMeasureSpec, int
heightMeasureSpec) {
  final int count = getChildCount();

  int maxHeight = 0;
  int maxWidth = 0;

  for (int i = 0; i < count; i++) {
    final View child = getChildAt(i);
    if (child.getVisibility() != GONE) {
      measureChild(child, widthMeasureSpec,
heightMeasureSpec);
    }
  }
  maxWidth += getPaddingLeft() + getPaddingRight();
  maxHeight += getPaddingTop() + getPaddingBottom();
  Drawable drawable = getBackground();
  if (drawable != null) {
    maxHeight = Math.max(maxHeight,
drawable.getMinimumHeight());
    maxWidth = Math.max(maxWidth,
drawable.getMinimumWidth());
  }
  setMeasuredDimension(resolveSize(maxWidth,
widthMeasureSpec),
```

```
    resolveSize(maxHeight, heightMeasureSpec));
}
private void drawPict(Canvas canvas, int x, int y, int w, int h,
float sx,
    float sy) {
  canvas.save();
  canvas.translate(x, y);
  canvas.clipRect(0, 0, w, h);
  canvas.scale(0.5f, 0.5f);
  canvas.scale(sx, sy, w, h);
  canvas.drawPicture(mPicture);
  canvas.restore();
}


@Override
protected void dispatchDraw(Canvas canvas) {
  super.dispatchDraw(mPicture.beginRecording(getWidth(),
getHeight()));
  mPicture.endRecording();


  int x = getWidth() / 2;
  int y = getHeight() / 2;


  if (false) {
```

```
    canvas.drawPicture(mPicture);
   } else {
    drawPict(canvas, 0, 0, x, y, 1, 1);
    drawPict(canvas, x, 0, x, y, -1, 1);
    drawPict(canvas, 0, y, x, y, 1, -1);
    drawPict(canvas, x, y, x, y, -1, -1);
   }
  }


  @Override
  public ViewParent invalidateChildInParent(int[] location, Rect
  dirty) {
    location[0] = getLeft();
    location[1] = getTop();
    dirty.set(0, 0, getWidth(), getHeight());
    return getParent();
  }


  @Override
  protected void onLayout(boolean changed, int l, int t, int r, int b)
  {
    final int count = super.getChildCount();

    for (int i = 0; i < count; i++) {
```

```
final View child = getChildAt(i);
if (child.getVisibility() != GONE) {
  final int childLeft = getPaddingLeft();
  final int childTop = getPaddingTop();
  child.layout(childLeft, childTop,
      childLeft + child.getMeasuredWidth(),
      childTop + child.getMeasuredHeight());
}
}
}
}
```

II.   Hardware

1. Code for SDCard operation

a. Loading images from currently mounted sdcard

```
package app.test;
import android.app.Activity;
import android.graphics.BitmapFactory;
import android.graphics.drawable.Drawable;
import android.net.Uri;
import android.os.Bundle;
import android.widget.ImageView;


public class Test extends Activity {
```

```java
@Override
public void onCreate(Bundle savedInstanceState) {

    super.onCreate(savedInstanceState);

    setContentView(R.layout.main);

    ImageView                  imgView                =
(ImageView)findViewById(R.id.image3);



imgView.setImageDrawable(Drawable.createFromPath("/m
nt/sdcard/d.jpg") );
    }
}
```

```xml
//main.xml


<?xml version="1.0" encoding="utf-8"?>
<!-- This file is at /res/layout/list.xml -->
<LinearLayout
xmlns:android="http://schemas.android.com/apk/res/andr
oid"
   android:orientation="horizontal"
   android:layout_width="fill_parent"
android:layout_height="fill_parent">
  <LinearLayout
   android:orientation="vertical"
```

```
        android:layout_width="wrap_content"
android:layout_height="fill_parent">


  <ImageView android:id="@+id/image1"

      android:layout_width="wrap_content"
android:layout_height="wrap_content"

      android:src="@drawable/icon"

  />


  <ImageView android:id="@+id/image2"

      android:layout_width="125dip"
android:layout_height="25dip"

      android:src="#555555"

  />

</LinearLayout>

<LinearLayout

    android:orientation="vertical"

    android:layout_width="wrap_content"
android:layout_height="fill_parent">


  <ImageView android:id="@+id/image3"

      android:layout_width="wrap_content"
android:layout_height="wrap_content"

  />
```

```
<ImageView android:id="@+id/image4"

    android:layout_width="wrap_content"
android:layout_height="wrap_content"

    android:src="@drawable/icon"

    android:scaleType="centerInside"

    android:maxWidth="35dip"  android:maxHeight="50dip"

    />


    </LinearLayout>

    </LinearLayout>
```

b. Creating File in the SDcard

```
//package ping.utils;

import java.io.File;

import java.io.FileOutputStream;

import java.io.IOException;

import java.io.InputStream;

import java.io.OutputStream;

import java.io.StringReader;

import java.util.ArrayList;

import java.util.Iterator;
```

```
import java.util.List;

import javax.xml.parsers.SAXParserFactory;

import org.xml.sax.InputSource;
import org.xml.sax.XMLReader;

import android.os.Environment;

public class FileUtils {
  private String SDCardRoot;

  public FileUtils() {
    SDCardRoot = Environment.getExternalStorageDirectory()
      .getAbsolutePath()
      + "/";
    System.out.println("SD dir:" + SDCardRoot);
  }

  public File createFileInSDCard(String fileName, String dir)
    throws IOException {
    File file = new File(SDCardRoot + dir + File.separator + fileName);
```

```
file.createNewFile();
return file;
}


public File createSDDir(String dir) {
File dirFile = new File(SDCardRoot + dir + File.separator);
System.out.println("creat dir:" + dirFile.mkdirs());
return dirFile;
}


public boolean isFileExist(String fileName, String path) {
File file = new File(SDCardRoot + path + File.separator +
fileName);
return file.exists();
}


public File write2SDFromInput(String path, String fileName,
    InputStream input) {
File file = null;
OutputStream output = null;
try {
  createSDDir(path);
  file = createFileInSDCard(fileName, path);
```

```
output = new FileOutputStream(file);
byte buffer[] = new byte[4 * 1024];
int temp;
while ((temp = input.read(buffer)) != -1) {
  output.write(buffer, 0, temp);
}
output.flush();
} catch (Exception e) {
  e.printStackTrace();
} finally {
  try {
    output.close();
  } catch (Exception e) {
    e.printStackTrace();
  }
}

return file;
}


}
```

c. Getting the sdcard path

```java
import java.io.File;

import android.os.Environment;

class Common {
  public static String getSdcardPath() {
    File sdDir = null;
    boolean            sdCardExist        =
Environment.getExternalStorageState().equals(
      android.os.Environment.MEDIA_MOUNTED);
    if (sdCardExist) {
     sdDir = Environment.getExternalStorageDirectory();
    }

    return sdDir.toString() + "/";
  }
}
```

Managing Power

```java
package app.test;

import java.io.BufferedWriter;
import java.io.FileWriter;
```

```
import java.io.IOException;

import java.text.SimpleDateFormat;

import java.util.Date;

import android.app.Activity;

import android.content.BroadcastReceiver;

import android.content.Context;

import android.content.Intent;

import android.content.IntentFilter;

import android.hardware.Sensor;

import android.hardware.SensorEvent;

import android.hardware.SensorEventListener;

import android.hardware.SensorManager;

import android.os.Bundle;

import android.os.Environment;

import android.os.PowerManager;

import android.os.PowerManager.WakeLock;

import android.provider.Settings;

import android.util.Log;


public class Test extends Activity implements
SensorEventListener {

   private WakeLock mWakelock = null;

  private SensorManager mMgr;
```

```
private Sensor mAccel;

private BufferedWriter mLog;

final private SimpleDateFormat mTimeFormat = new
SimpleDateFormat("HH:mm:ss - ");

private int mSavedTimeout;


@Override
public void onCreate(Bundle savedInstanceState) {

    super.onCreate(savedInstanceState);

    setContentView(R.layout.main);

    mMgr                    =            (SensorManager)
this.getSystemService(SENSOR_SERVICE);

    mAccel                                            =
mMgr.getDefaultSensor(Sensor.TYPE_ACCELEROMETER);

    try {

    String              filename              =
Environment.getExternalStorageDirectory().getAbsolutePath()
+"/accel.log";

        mLog = new BufferedWriter(new FileWriter(filename,
true));

    }

    catch(Exception e) {

      e.printStackTrace();

      finish();

    }
```

```
PowerManager pwrMgr = (PowerManager)
this.getSystemService(POWER_SERVICE);

mWakelock =
pwrMgr.newWakeLock(PowerManager.PARTIAL_WAKE_LO
CK, "Accel");

mWakelock.acquire();


try {

mSavedTimeout =
Settings.System.getInt(getContentResolver(),

    Settings.System.SCREEN_OFF_TIMEOUT);

}

catch(Exception e) {

mSavedTimeout = 120000;

}

Settings.System.putInt(getContentResolver(),

    Settings.System.SCREEN_OFF_TIMEOUT, 5000);

}


public BroadcastReceiver mReceiver = new
BroadcastReceiver() {

public void onReceive(Context context, Intent intent) {

    if
(Intent.ACTION_SCREEN_OFF.equals(intent.getAction())) {
```

```
        writeLog("The screen has turned off");

        mMgr.unregisterListener(Test.this);

        mMgr.registerListener(Test.this, mAccel,

          SensorManager.SENSOR_DELAY_NORMAL);

      }

    }

  };

  @Override

  protected void onStart() {

    mMgr.registerListener(this,                    mAccel,
SensorManager.SENSOR_DELAY_NORMAL);

    IntentFilter              filter            =              new
IntentFilter(Intent.ACTION_SCREEN_OFF);

    registerReceiver(mReceiver, filter);

   super.onStart();

  }

  @Override

  protected void onStop() {

    mMgr.unregisterListener(this, mAccel);

    unregisterReceiver(mReceiver);

    try {

   mLog.flush();

  } catch (IOException e) {

  }
```

```
  super.onStop();
 }
 @Override
 protected void onDestroy() {
  try {
    mLog.flush();
    mLog.close();
  }
  catch(Exception e) {
  }
    Settings.System.putInt(getContentResolver(),
        Settings.System.SCREEN_OFF_TIMEOUT,
mSavedTimeout);
    mWakelock.release();
    super.onDestroy();
 }
public void onAccuracyChanged(Sensor sensor, int accuracy) {
}
public void onSensorChanged(SensorEvent event) {
  writeLog("Got a sensor event: " + event.values[0] + ", " +
    event.values[1] + ", " + event.values[2]);
}
private void writeLog(String str) {
```

```
try {
    Date now = new Date();
    mLog.write(mTimeFormat.format(now));
   mLog.write(str);
   mLog.write("\n");
  }
  catch(IOException ioe) {
   ioe.printStackTrace();
  }
 }
}
```

Retrieving your memory information
package app.test;

import java.io.BufferedWriter;
import java.io.FileWriter;
import java.io.IOException;
import java.text.SimpleDateFormat;
import java.util.Date;
import android.app.Activity;
import android.content.BroadcastReceiver;
import android.content.Context;

```
import android.content.Intent;

import android.content.IntentFilter;

import android.hardware.Sensor;

import android.hardware.SensorEvent;

import android.hardware.SensorEventListener;

import android.hardware.SensorManager;

import android.os.Bundle;

import android.os.Environment;

import android.os.PowerManager;

import android.os.PowerManager.WakeLock;

import android.provider.Settings;

import android.util.Log;


public class Test extends Activity implements SensorEventListener {
    private WakeLock mWakelock = null;

   private SensorManager mMgr;

    private Sensor mAccel;

    private BufferedWriter mLog;

   final private SimpleDateFormat mTimeFormat = new SimpleDateFormat("HH:mm:ss - ");

   private int mSavedTimeout;


   @Override
```

```
public void onCreate(Bundle savedInstanceState) {

    super.onCreate(savedInstanceState);

    setContentView(R.layout.main);

    mMgr                    =              (SensorManager)
    this.getSystemService(SENSOR_SERVICE);

    mAccel                                                =
    mMgr.getDefaultSensor(Sensor.TYPE_ACCELEROMETER);

    try {

        String              filename           =
    Environment.getExternalStorageDirectory().getAbsolutePath()
    +"/accel.log";

        mLog = new BufferedWriter(new FileWriter(filename,
    true));

    }

    catch(Exception e) {

     e.printStackTrace();

     finish();

    }


    PowerManager     pwrMgr     =     (PowerManager)
    this.getSystemService(POWER_SERVICE);

    mWakelock                                            =
    pwrMgr.newWakeLock(PowerManager.PARTIAL_WAKE_LO
    CK, "Accel");

    mWakelock.acquire();
```

```
try {
mSavedTimeout                                            =
Settings.System.getInt(getContentResolver(),
      Settings.System.SCREEN_OFF_TIMEOUT);
}
catch(Exception e) {
  mSavedTimeout = 120000;
}
Settings.System.putInt(getContentResolver(),
    Settings.System.SCREEN_OFF_TIMEOUT, 5000);
}


public      BroadcastReceiver      mReceiver    =      new
BroadcastReceiver() {
    public void onReceive(Context context, Intent intent) {
    if
(Intent.ACTION_SCREEN_OFF.equals(intent.getAction())) {
      writeLog("The screen has turned off");
      mMgr.unregisterListener(Test.this);
      mMgr.registerListener(Test.this, mAccel,
        SensorManager.SENSOR_DELAY_NORMAL);
    }
  }
};
```

```
@Override

protected void onStart() {

    mMgr.registerListener(this,                    mAccel,
SensorManager.SENSOR_DELAY_NORMAL);

    IntentFilter           filter        =          new
IntentFilter(Intent.ACTION_SCREEN_OFF);

    registerReceiver(mReceiver, filter);

  super.onStart();

}

@Override

protected void onStop() {

  mMgr.unregisterListener(this, mAccel);

  unregisterReceiver(mReceiver);

  try {

 mLog.flush();

} catch (IOException e) {

}

  super.onStop();

}

@Override

protected void onDestroy() {

  try {

    mLog.flush();

    mLog.close();
```

```
    }
    catch(Exception e) {
    }
      Settings.System.putInt(getContentResolver(),
          Settings.System.SCREEN_OFF_TIMEOUT,
mSavedTimeout);
      mWakelock.release();
      super.onDestroy();
  }
  public void onAccuracyChanged(Sensor sensor, int accuracy) {
  }
  public void onSensorChanged(SensorEvent event) {
    writeLog("Got a sensor event: " + event.values[0] + ", " +
      event.values[1] + ", " + event.values[2]);
  }
  private void writeLog(String str) {
    try {
      Date now = new Date();
      mLog.write(mTimeFormat.format(now));
      mLog.write(str);
      mLog.write("\n");
    }
    catch(IOException ioe) {
```

```
    ioe.printStackTrace();
  }
 }
}
```

Computing the Total Memory

//package org.anddev.andengine.util;

```
import java.io.IOException;
import java.io.InputStream;
import java.lang.reflect.Method;
import java.util.Scanner;
import java.util.regex.MatchResult;


import android.content.Context;
import android.content.pm.PackageInfo;
import android.content.pm.PackageManager;
import android.content.pm.PackageManager.NameNotFoundException;
import android.os.Build;


/**
 * (c) 2010 Nicolas Gramlich
```

```
 * (c) 2011 Zynga Inc.
 *
 * @author Nicolas Gramlich
 * @since 15:50:31 - 14.07.2010
 */
class SystemUtils {

  private static final String BOGOMIPS_PATTERN =
"BogoMIPS[\\s]*:[\\s]*(\\d+\\.\\d+)[\\s]*\n";

  private static final String MEMTOTAL_PATTERN =
"MemTotal[\\s]*:[\\s]*(\\d+)[\\s]*kB\n";

  private static final String MEMFREE_PATTERN =
"MemFree[\\s]*:[\\s]*(\\d+)[\\s]*kB\n";



  /**
   * @return in kiloBytes.
   * @throws SystemUtilsException
   */
  public static int getMemoryTotal() throws Exception {

    final MatchResult matchResult =
SystemUtils.matchSystemFile("/proc/meminfo",
MEMTOTAL_PATTERN, 1000);


    try {

      if(matchResult.groupCount() > 0) {
```

```
    return Integer.parseInt(matchResult.group(1));
  } else {
    throw new Exception();
  }
  } catch (final NumberFormatException e) {
    throw new Exception(e);
  }
}
```

```
  private static MatchResult matchSystemFile(final String
pSystemFile, final String pPattern, final int pHorizon) throws
Exception {
    InputStream in = null;
    try {
      final Process process = new ProcessBuilder(new String[] {
"/system/bin/cat", pSystemFile }).start();


      in = process.getInputStream();
      final Scanner scanner = new Scanner(in);


      final           boolean          matchFound          =
scanner.findWithinHorizon(pPattern, pHorizon) != null;
      if(matchFound) {
        return scanner.match();
```

```
    } else {
      throw new Exception();
    }
  } catch (final IOException e) {
    throw new Exception(e);
  }


 }
}
```

Computing Free Memory

//package org.anddev.andengine.util;

```
import java.io.IOException;
import java.io.InputStream;
import java.lang.reflect.Method;
import java.util.Scanner;
import java.util.regex.MatchResult;

import android.content.Context;
import android.content.pm.PackageInfo;
import android.content.pm.PackageManager;
```

```java
import
android.content.pm.PackageManager.NameNotFoundExceptio
n;

import android.os.Build;


/**
 * (c) 2010 Nicolas Gramlich
 * (c) 2011 Zynga Inc.
 *
 * @author Nicolas Gramlich
 * @since 15:50:31 - 14.07.2010
 */
class SystemUtils {
 private static final String BOGOMIPS_PATTERN =
"BogoMIPS[\\s]*:[\\s]*(\\d+\\.\\d+)[\\s]*\n";

 private static final String MEMTOTAL_PATTERN =
"MemTotal[\\s]*:[\\s]*(\\d+)[\\s]*kB\n";

 private static final String MEMFREE_PATTERN =
"MemFree[\\s]*:[\\s]*(\\d+)[\\s]*kB\n";



 /**
  * @return in kiloBytes.
  * @throws SystemUtilsException
  */
```

```
public static int getMemoryFree() throws Exception {

  final          MatchResult          matchResult          =
SystemUtils.matchSystemFile("/proc/meminfo",
MEMFREE_PATTERN, 1000);


  try {
    if(matchResult.groupCount() > 0) {
      return Integer.parseInt(matchResult.group(1));
    } else {
      throw new Exception();
    }
  } catch (final NumberFormatException e) {
    throw new Exception(e);
  }
}

  private   static   MatchResult   matchSystemFile(final   String
pSystemFile, final String pPattern, final int pHorizon) throws
Exception {

  InputStream in = null;

  try {

    final Process process = new ProcessBuilder(new String[] {
"/system/bin/cat", pSystemFile }).start();


    in = process.getInputStream();

    final Scanner scanner = new Scanner(in);
```

```
final          boolean          matchFound          =
scanner.findWithinHorizon(pPattern, pHorizon) != null;

   if(matchFound) {

    return scanner.match();

   } else {

    throw new Exception();

   }

   } catch (final IOException e) {

    throw new Exception(e);

   }


  }
 }
```

III. UI (User Interface)

a. Programming action bar tabs and their interaction with action bar features

```
/*

 * Copyright (C) 2010 The Android Open Source Project

 *

 * Licensed under the Apache License, Version 2.0 (the
"License");
```

```
* you may not use this file except in compliance with the
License.

* You may obtain a copy of the License at
*

*    http://www.apache.org/licenses/LICENSE-2.0
*

* Unless required by applicable law or agreed to in writing,
software

* distributed under the License is distributed on an "AS IS"
BASIS,

* WITHOUT WARRANTIES OR CONDITIONS OF ANY KIND,
either express or implied.

* See the License for the specific language governing
permissions and

* limitations under the License.

*/
package app.test;

import android.app.ActionBar;

import android.app.ActionBar.Tab;

import android.app.Activity;

import android.app.Fragment;

import android.app.FragmentTransaction;

import android.os.Bundle;

import android.view.LayoutInflater;

import android.view.View;
```

```java
import android.view.ViewGroup;
import android.widget.TextView;
import android.widget.Toast;

/**
 * This demonstrates the use of action bar tabs and how they interact
 * with other action bar features.
 */
public class Test extends Activity {
  @Override
  protected void onCreate(Bundle savedInstanceState) {
    super.onCreate(savedInstanceState);

    setContentView(R.layout.main);
  }

  public void onAddTab(View v) {
    final ActionBar bar = getActionBar();
    final int tabCount = bar.getTabCount();
    final String text = "Tab " + tabCount;
    bar.addTab(bar.newTab()
        .setText(text)
```

```
        .setTabListener(new TabListener(new
TabContentFragment(text))));
    }


    public void onRemoveTab(View v) {
      final ActionBar bar = getActionBar();
      bar.removeTabAt(bar.getTabCount() - 1);
    }


    public void onToggleTabs(View v) {
      final ActionBar bar = getActionBar();


      if (bar.getNavigationMode() ==
ActionBar.NAVIGATION_MODE_TABS) {


bar.setNavigationMode(ActionBar.NAVIGATION_MODE_STA
NDARD);


bar.setDisplayOptions(ActionBar.DISPLAY_SHOW_TITLE,
ActionBar.DISPLAY_SHOW_TITLE);
        } else {


bar.setNavigationMode(ActionBar.NAVIGATION_MODE_TA
BS);


        bar.setDisplayOptions(0,
ActionBar.DISPLAY_SHOW_TITLE);
```

```
    }
}


public void onRemoveAllTabs(View v) {

    getActionBar().removeAllTabs();

}


/**
```

* A TabListener receives event callbacks from the action bar as tabs

* are deselected, selected, and reselected. A FragmentTransaction

* is provided to each of these callbacks; if any operations are added

* to it, it will be committed at the end of the full tab switch operation.

* This lets tab switches be atomic without the app needing to track

* the interactions between different tabs.

*

* NOTE: This is a very simple implementation that does not retain

* fragment state of the non-visible tabs across activity instances.

* Look at the FragmentTabs example for how to do a more complete

```
 * implementation.
 */
private class TabListener implements ActionBar.TabListener
{
    private TabContentFragment mFragment;

    public TabListener(TabContentFragment fragment) {
        mFragment = fragment;
    }

    public void onTabSelected(Tab tab, FragmentTransaction
ft) {
        ft.add(R.id.fragment_content, mFragment,
mFragment.getText());
    }

    public void onTabUnselected(Tab tab,
FragmentTransaction ft) {
        ft.remove(mFragment);
    }

    public void onTabReselected(Tab tab,
FragmentTransaction ft) {
        Toast.makeText(Test.this, "Reselected!",
Toast.LENGTH_SHORT).show();
```

```
    }

  }


  private class TabContentFragment extends Fragment {
    private String mText;

    public TabContentFragment(String text) {
      mText = text;
    }

    public String getText() {
      return mText;
    }


    @Override
    public View onCreateView(LayoutInflater inflater,
ViewGroup container,
        Bundle savedInstanceState) {
        View fragView = inflater.inflate(R.layout.row, container,
false);


      TextView text = (TextView)
fragView.findViewById(R.id.text);
```

```
text.setText(mText);

return fragView;
    }


  }
}
//main.xml
```

```xml
<?xml version="1.0" encoding="utf-8"?>
<!-- Copyright (C) 2010 The Android Open Source Project


    Licensed under the Apache License, Version 2.0 (the
"License");
    you may not use this file except in compliance with the
License.
    You may obtain a copy of the License at


        http://www.apache.org/licenses/LICENSE-2.0


    Unless required by applicable law or agreed to in writing,
software
    distributed under the License is distributed on an "AS IS"
BASIS,
```

WITHOUT WARRANTIES OR CONDITIONS OF ANY KIND, either express or implied.

See the License for the specific language governing permissions and

limitations under the License.

```
-->
<LinearLayout
xmlns:android="http://schemas.android.com/apk/res/android"
        android:layout_width="match_parent"
        android:layout_height="match_parent"
        android:orientation="vertical">
    <FrameLayout android:id="@+id/fragment_content"
        android:layout_width="match_parent"
        android:layout_height="0dip"
        android:layout_weight="1" />
    <LinearLayout android:layout_width="match_parent"
        android:layout_height="0dip"
        android:layout_weight="1"
        android:orientation="vertical">
      <Button android:id="@+id/btn_add_tab"
        android:layout_width="wrap_content"
        android:layout_height="wrap_content"
        android:text="btn_add_tab"
```

```xml
        android:onClick="onAddTab" />
    <Button android:id="@+id/btn_remove_tab"
        android:layout_width="wrap_content"
        android:layout_height="wrap_content"
        android:text="btn_remove_tab"
        android:onClick="onRemoveTab" />
    <Button android:id="@+id/btn_toggle_tabs"
        android:layout_width="wrap_content"
        android:layout_height="wrap_content"
        android:text="btn_toggle_tabs"
        android:onClick="onToggleTabs" />
    <Button android:id="@+id/btn_remove_all_tabs"
        android:layout_width="wrap_content"
        android:layout_height="wrap_content"
        android:text="btn_remove_all_tabs"
        android:onClick="onRemoveAllTabs" />
    </LinearLayout>
</LinearLayout>
```

//row.xml

```xml
<?xml version="1.0" encoding="utf-8"?>
```

<!-- Copyright (C) 2010 The Android Open Source Project

   Licensed under the Apache License, Version 2.0 (the "License");

   you may not use this file except in compliance with the License.

   You may obtain a copy of the License at

     http://www.apache.org/licenses/LICENSE-2.0

   Unless required by applicable law or agreed to in writing, software

   distributed under the License is distributed on an "AS IS" BASIS,

   WITHOUT WARRANTIES OR CONDITIONS OF ANY KIND, either express or implied.

   See the License for the specific language governing permissions and

   limitations under the License.
-->
<TextView xmlns:android="http://schemas.android.com/apk/res/android"

     android:id="@+id/text"

     android:layout_width="wrap_content"

     android:layout_height="wrap_content" />

2. Clocks: Digital and Analog

```
package app.test;
import android.app.Activity;
import android.os.Bundle;
public class Test extends Activity {
  @Override
  public void onCreate(Bundle icicle) {
    super.onCreate(icicle);
    setContentView(R.layout.main);
  }
}
//main.xml
<?xml version="1.0" encoding="utf-8"?>
<RelativeLayout
xmlns:android="http://schemas.android.com/apk/res/android"
  android:orientation="vertical"
  android:layout_width="fill_parent"
  android:layout_height="fill_parent"
  >
  <AnalogClock android:id="@+id/analog"
    android:layout_width="fill_parent"
    android:layout_height="wrap_content"
```

```
android:layout_centerHorizontal="true"
android:layout_alignParentTop="true"
/>
<DigitalClock android:id="@+id/digital"
android:layout_width="wrap_content"
android:layout_height="wrap_content"
android:layout_centerHorizontal="true"
android:layout_below="@id/analog"
/>
</RelativeLayout>
```

IV. All About the Menu

1. Creating your Option menu

```
package app.Test;


import android.app.Activity;
import android.app.AlertDialog;
import android.content.DialogInterface;
import android.os.Bundle;
import android.view.Menu;
import android.view.MenuInflater;
import android.view.MenuItem;
import android.widget.ImageView;
```

```
import android.widget.LinearLayout;

public class appTest extends Activity {
  @Override
  public void onCreate(Bundle savedInstanceState) {
    super.onCreate(savedInstanceState);
    setContentView(R.layout.main);
  }

  public boolean onCreateOptionsMenu(Menu menu) {
    MenuInflater inflater = getMenuInflater();
    inflater.inflate(R.menu.mainmenu, menu);
    return true;
  }

  public boolean onOptionsItemSelected(MenuItem item) {
    LinearLayout bkgr = (LinearLayout)
findViewById(R.id.uilayout);

    final ImageView image = (ImageView)
findViewById(R.id.ImageView01);


    AlertDialog.Builder builder = new
AlertDialog.Builder(this);
```

```
builder.setTitle("Pick an Image!")
   .setMessage("Please Select Image One or Image Two:")
   .setCancelable(false)
   .setPositiveButton("IMAGE 1",
      new DialogInterface.OnClickListener() {
         public void onClick(DialogInterface dialog, int id) {
            image.setImageResource(R.drawable.image1);
         }
      })

   .setNegativeButton("IMAGE 2",
      new DialogInterface.OnClickListener() {
         public void onClick(DialogInterface dialog, int id) {
            image.setImageResource(R.drawable.image2);
         }
      });

switch (item.getItemId()) {
case R.id.buttonone:
   image.setImageResource(R.drawable.image1);
   return true;
case R.id.buttontwo:
   image.setImageResource(R.drawable.image2);
```

```
   return true;
 case R.id.buttonthree:
 bkgr.setBackgroundResource(R.color.background2);
   return true;
 case R.id.buttonfour:
 bkgr.setBackgroundResource(R.color.background);
   return true;
 case R.id.buttonfive:
 builder.show();
   return true;
 default:
 return super.onOptionsItemSelected(item);
 }
 }
}
```

//main.xml

```xml
<?xml version="1.0" encoding="utf-8"?>
<LinearLayout
xmlns:android="http://schemas.android.com/apk/res/andr
oid"
 android:id="@+id/uilayout"
  android:orientation="vertical"
```

```
android:layout_width="fill_parent"
android:layout_height="fill_parent"
android:background="@color/background">


<ImageButton android:id="@+id/button_one"
    android:layout_width="wrap_content"
    android:layout_height="wrap_content"
    android:src="@drawable/button1"
    android:paddingTop="5px"
    android:background="#00000000">
</ImageButton>


<TextView  android:id="@+id/TextView01"
    android:layout_width="wrap_content"
    android:layout_height="wrap_content"
    android:text="Sample Text"
    android:textColor="#CCCC77"
    android:padding="12dip">
</TextView>


<ImageView  android:id="@+id/ImageView01"
    android:layout_width="wrap_content"
    android:layout_height="wrap_content"
```

```
    android:src="@drawable/image1">
  </ImageView>


</LinearLayout>


//mainmenu.xml
<?xml version="1.0" encoding="utf-8"?>


<menu
xmlns:android="http://schemas.android.com/apk/res/andr
oid">

  <item android:id="@+id/buttonone"
    android:icon="@drawable/image1icon"
    android:title="@string/showimage1" />

  <item android:id="@+id/buttontwo"
    android:icon="@drawable/image2icon"
    android:title="@string/showimage2" />

  <item android:id="@+id/buttonthree"
    android:icon="@drawable/menu3icon"
    android:title="@string/showwhite" />
```

```
<item android:id="@+id/buttonfour"
    android:icon="@drawable/menu4icon"
    android:title="@string/showblack" />

<item android:id="@+id/buttonfive"
    android:icon="@drawable/menu5icon"
    android:title="@string/showalert" />

</menu>
```

2. Your Messages Menu

```
/*
```

Welcome to the source code for Android Programming Tutorials (http://commonsware.com/AndTutorials)!

Specifically, this is for Version 3.2 and above of this book. For the source code for older versions of this book, please visit:

https://github.com/commonsguy/cw-andtutorials

All of the source code in this archive is licensed under the

Apache 2.0 license except as noted.

The names of the top-level directories roughly correspond to a

shortened form of the chapter titles. Since chapter numbers

change with every release, and since some samples are used by

multiple chapters, I am loathe to put chapter numbers in the

actual directory names.

If you wish to use this code, bear in mind a few things:

* The projects are set up to be built by Ant, not by Eclipse.

  If you wish to use the code with Eclipse, you will need to

  create a suitable Android Eclipse project and import the

  code and other assets.

* You should delete build.xml from the project, then run

  android update project -p ...

  (where ... is the path to a project of interest)

  on those projects you wish to use, so the build files are

  updated for your Android SDK version.

```
*/


package apt.tutorial;

import android.app.TabActivity;
import android.os.Bundle;
import android.view.Menu;
import android.view.MenuInflater;
import android.view.MenuItem;
import android.view.View;
import android.view.ViewGroup;
import android.view.LayoutInflater;
import android.widget.AdapterView;
import android.widget.ArrayAdapter;
import android.widget.Button;
import android.widget.EditText;
import android.widget.ImageView;
import android.widget.ListView;
import android.widget.RadioGroup;
import android.widget.TabHost;
import android.widget.TextView;
```

```
import android.widget.Toast;
import java.util.ArrayList;
import java.util.List;


public class LunchList extends TabActivity {
  List<Restaurant> model=new ArrayList<Restaurant>();
  RestaurantAdapter adapter=null;
  EditText name=null;
  EditText address=null;
  EditText notes=null;
  RadioGroup types=null;
  Restaurant current=null;

  @Override
  public void onCreate(Bundle savedInstanceState) {
    super.onCreate(savedInstanceState);
    setContentView(R.layout.main);

    name=(EditText)findViewById(R.id.name);
    address=(EditText)findViewById(R.id.addr);
    notes=(EditText)findViewById(R.id.notes);
    types=(RadioGroup)findViewById(R.id.types);
```

```
Button save=(Button)findViewById(R.id.save);

save.setOnClickListener(onSave);

ListView list=(ListView)findViewById(R.id.restaurants);

adapter=new RestaurantAdapter();
list.setAdapter(adapter);

TabHost.TabSpec
spec=getTabHost().newTabSpec("tag1");

spec.setContent(R.id.restaurants);
spec.setIndicator("List", getResources()
                .getDrawable(R.drawable.list));
getTabHost().addTab(spec);

spec=getTabHost().newTabSpec("tag2");
spec.setContent(R.id.details);
spec.setIndicator("Details", getResources()
                .getDrawable(R.drawable.restaurant));
getTabHost().addTab(spec);
```

```
getTabHost().setCurrentTab(o);

list.setOnItemClickListener(onListClick);
}

@Override
public boolean onCreateOptionsMenu(Menu menu) {
  new MenuInflater(this).inflate(R.menu.option, menu);

  return(super.onCreateOptionsMenu(menu));
}

@Override
public boolean onOptionsItemSelected(MenuItem item) {
  if (item.getItemId()==R.id.toast) {
    String message="No restaurant selected";

    if (current!=null) {
      message=current.getNotes();
    }

    Toast.makeText(this, message,
Toast.LENGTH_LONG).show();
```

```
    return(true);
  }


  return(super.onOptionsItemSelected(item));
}


private View.OnClickListener onSave=new
View.OnClickListener() {
  public void onClick(View v) {
    current=new Restaurant();
    current.setName(name.getText().toString());
    current.setAddress(address.getText().toString());
    current.setNotes(notes.getText().toString());

    switch (types.getCheckedRadioButtonId()) {
      case R.id.sit_down:
        current.setType("sit_down");
        break;

      case R.id.take_out:
        current.setType("take_out");
        break;
```

```
    case R.id.delivery:
      current.setType("delivery");
      break;
  }


  adapter.add(current);
  }
};


private AdapterView.OnItemClickListener onListClick=new
AdapterView.OnItemClickListener() {
  public void onItemClick(AdapterView<?> parent,
                  View view, int position,
                  long id) {
    current=model.get(position);

    name.setText(current.getName());
    address.setText(current.getAddress());
    notes.setText(current.getNotes());

    if (current.getType().equals("sit_down")) {
      types.check(R.id.sit_down);
```

```
    }
    else if (current.getType().equals("take_out")) {
      types.check(R.id.take_out);
    }
    else {
      types.check(R.id.delivery);
    }


    getTabHost().setCurrentTab(1);
    }
  };


  class RestaurantAdapter extends
ArrayAdapter<Restaurant> {
    RestaurantAdapter() {
      super(LunchList.this, R.layout.row, model);
    }


    public View getView(int position, View convertView,
            ViewGroup parent) {
      View row=convertView;
      RestaurantHolder holder=null;
```

```
if (row==null) {
  LayoutInflater inflater=getLayoutInflater();

  row=inflater.inflate(R.layout.row, parent, false);
  holder=new RestaurantHolder(row);
  row.setTag(holder);
}
else {
  holder=(RestaurantHolder)row.getTag();
}

holder.populateFrom(model.get(position));

return(row);
}
}

static class RestaurantHolder {
  private TextView name=null;
  private TextView address=null;
  private ImageView icon=null;

  RestaurantHolder(View row) {
```

```
name=(TextView)row.findViewById(R.id.title);
address=(TextView)row.findViewById(R.id.address);
icon=(ImageView)row.findViewById(R.id.icon);
}

void populateFrom(Restaurant r) {
name.setText(r.getName());
address.setText(r.getAddress());

if (r.getType().equals("sit_down")) {
  icon.setImageResource(R.drawable.ball_red);
}
else if (r.getType().equals("take_out")) {
  icon.setImageResource(R.drawable.ball_yellow);
}
else {
  icon.setImageResource(R.drawable.ball_green);
}
}
}
}
```

```
package apt.tutorial;

public class Restaurant {
  private String name="";
  private String address="";
  private String type="";
  private String notes="";

  public String getName() {
   return(name);
  }

  public void setName(String name) {
   this.name=name;
  }

  public String getAddress() {
   return(address);
  }

  public void setAddress(String address) {
   this.address=address;
  }
```

```
public String getType() {
  return(type);
}

public void setType(String type) {
  this.type=type;
}

public String getNotes() {
  return(notes);
}

public void setNotes(String notes) {
  this.notes=notes;
}

public String toString() {
  return(getName());
}
}
```

//strings.xml

```xml
<?xml version="1.0" encoding="utf-8"?>
<resources>
    <string name="app_name">LunchList</string>
</resources>
```

//option.xml

```xml
<?xml version="1.0" encoding="utf-8"?>
<menu xmlns:android="http://schemas.android.com/apk/res/android">
    <item android:id="@+id/toast"
      android:title="Raise Toast"
      android:icon="@drawable/toast"
    />
</menu>
```

//main.xml

```xml
<?xml version="1.0" encoding="utf-8"?>
```

```xml
<TabHost
xmlns:android="http://schemas.android.com/apk/res/android"
 android:id="@android:id/tabhost"
 android:layout_width="fill_parent"
 android:layout_height="fill_parent">
 <LinearLayout
  android:orientation="vertical"
  android:layout_width="fill_parent"
  android:layout_height="fill_parent">
  <TabWidget android:id="@android:id/tabs"
   android:layout_width="fill_parent"
   android:layout_height="wrap_content"
 />
  <FrameLayout android:id="@android:id/tabcontent"
   android:layout_width="fill_parent"
   android:layout_height="fill_parent"
 >
   <ListView android:id="@+id/restaurants"
    android:layout_width="fill_parent"
    android:layout_height="fill_parent"
  />
   <TableLayout android:id="@+id/details"
    android:layout_width="fill_parent"
```

```
android:layout_height="wrap_content"
android:stretchColumns="1"
android:paddingTop="4dip"
>
<TableRow>
  <TextView android:text="Name:" />
  <EditText android:id="@+id/name" />
</TableRow>
<TableRow>
  <TextView android:text="Address:" />
  <EditText android:id="@+id/addr" />
</TableRow>
<TableRow>
  <TextView android:text="Type:" />
  <RadioGroup android:id="@+id/types">
   <RadioButton android:id="@+id/take_out"
    android:text="Take-Out"
   />
   <RadioButton android:id="@+id/sit_down"
    android:text="Sit-Down"
   />
   <RadioButton android:id="@+id/delivery"
    android:text="Delivery"
```

```
      />
     </RadioGroup>
    </TableRow>
    <TableRow>
     <TextView android:text="Notes:" />
     <EditText android:id="@+id/notes"
      android:singleLine="false"
      android:gravity="top"
      android:lines="2"
      android:scrollHorizontally="false"
      android:maxLines="2"
      android:maxWidth="200sp"
     />
    </TableRow>
    <Button android:id="@+id/save"
      android:layout_width="fill_parent"
      android:layout_height="wrap_content"
      android:text="Save"
     />
   </TableLayout>
  </FrameLayout>
 </LinearLayout>
</TabHost>
```

//row.xml

```xml
<LinearLayout
xmlns:android="http://schemas.android.com/apk/res/android"
  android:layout_width="fill_parent"
  android:layout_height="wrap_content"
  android:orientation="horizontal"
  android:padding="4dip"
  >
  <ImageView android:id="@+id/icon"
    android:layout_width="wrap_content"
    android:layout_height="fill_parent"
    android:layout_alignParentTop="true"
    android:layout_alignParentBottom="true"
    android:layout_marginRight="4dip"
  />
  <LinearLayout
    android:layout_width="fill_parent"
    android:layout_height="wrap_content"
    android:orientation="vertical"
    >
    <TextView android:id="@+id/title"
```

```
        android:layout_width="fill_parent"
        android:layout_height="wrap_content"
        android:layout_weight="1"
        android:gravity="center_vertical"
        android:textStyle="bold"
        android:singleLine="true"
        android:ellipsize="end"
    />
    <TextView android:id="@+id/address"
        android:layout_width="fill_parent"
        android:layout_height="wrap_content"
        android:layout_weight="1"
        android:gravity="center_vertical"
        android:singleLine="true"
        android:ellipsize="end"
    />
  </LinearLayout>
</LinearLayout>
```

V. Core Class

1. Your Timer Table

```
import java.util.HashMap;
```

```
class MyTimer {

  // WARNING: HashMap is not thread-safe (not
syncronized)

  static private HashMap<String, MyTimer> timers = new
HashMap<String, MyTimer>();


  private String name = null;


  private long startedAt;

  private long elapsedTimeInMS = 0;



  static public MyTimer get(String name) {
    MyTimer timer;
    if (timers.containsKey(name)) {
      timer = timers.get(name);
    } else {
      timer = new MyTimer(name);
      timers.put(name, timer);
    }
    return timer;
  }
```

```
/**
 * If given a name the timer will be save in the list
 * @param name
 * @return
 */
static public MyTimer start(String name) {
  MyTimer timer = get(name);
  timer.start();
  return timer;
}


static public MyTimer resume(String name) {
  MyTimer timer = get(name);
  timer.resume();
  return timer;
}


static public MyTimer stop(String name) {
  MyTimer timer = get(name);
  timer.stop();
  return timer;
}
```

```java
static public MyTimer remove(String name) {
  return timers.remove(name);
}



// Private constructor prevents instantiation
private MyTimer(String name) {
  this.name = name;
}

public void start() {
  this.elapsedTimeInMS = 0;
  this.startedAt = System.currentTimeMillis();
}

public void resume() {
  this.startedAt = System.currentTimeMillis();
}

/**
 * @return elapsedTimeInMS
 */
public long stop() {
```

```
  this.elapsedTimeInMS += (System.currentTimeMillis() -
this.startedAt);
  return this.elapsedTimeInMS;
}


public long ms() {
  return this.elapsedTimeInMS;
}


public float seconds() {
  return this.elapsedTimeInMS / 1000F;
}


public String name() { return this.name; }


/**
 * Adds the value of another timer to this one
 * @param otherTimer
 */
public MyTimer add(MyTimer otherTimer) {
  this.elapsedTimeInMS += otherTimer.ms();
  return this;
}
```

```
public MyTimer add(String name) {
  this.elapsedTimeInMS += get(name).ms();
  return this;
}

public String toString() {
  return Float.toString(seconds()) + "s";
  }
}
```

2. Code for the Use of Google Maps

//AndroidManifest.xml

```
<?xml version="1.0" encoding="utf-8"?>
<manifest
xmlns:android="http://schemas.android.com/apk/res/andr
oid"
    package="com.examples.mapper"
    android:versionCode="1"
    android:versionName="1.0">
  <uses-sdk android:minSdkVersion="3" />
```

```
    <uses-permission
android:name="android.permission.ACCESS_FINE_LOCAT
ION"></uses-permission>

    <uses-permission
android:name="android.permission.INTERNET"></uses-
permission>


    <application android:icon="@drawable/icon"
android:label="@string/app_name">

    <activity android:name=".MyActivity"

        android:label="@string/app_name">

    <intent-filter>

    <action
android:name="android.intent.action.MAIN" />

        <category
android:name="android.intent.category.LAUNCHER" />

    </intent-filter>

    </activity>

    <uses-library
android:name="com.google.android.maps"></uses-library>


    </application>

</manifest>


//main.xml
```

```xml
<?xml version="1.0" encoding="utf-8"?>
<LinearLayout
xmlns:android="http://schemas.android.com/apk/res/android"
 android:orientation="vertical"
 android:layout_width="fill_parent"
 android:layout_height="fill_parent">
 <TextView
  android:layout_width="fill_parent"
  android:layout_height="wrap_content"
  android:gravity="center_horizontal"
  android:text="Map Of Your Location"
 />
 <com.google.android.maps.MapView
  android:id="@+id/map"
  android:layout_width="fill_parent"
  android:layout_height="fill_parent"
  android:enabled="true"
  android:clickable="true"
  android:apiKey="YOUR_API_KEY_HERE"
 />
</LinearLayout>
```

```java
package app.test;
```

```
import android.os.Bundle;

import com.google.android.maps.MapActivity;
import com.google.android.maps.MapController;
import com.google.android.maps.MapView;

public class MyActivity extends MapActivity {

  MapView map;
  MapController controller;

  @Override
  public void onCreate(Bundle savedInstanceState) {
    super.onCreate(savedInstanceState);
    setContentView(R.layout.main);

    map = (MapView)findViewById(R.id.map);
    controller = map.getController();

    LocationManager manager =
(LocationManager)getSystemService(Context.LOCATION_S
ERVICE);
```

```java
Location location =
manager.getLastKnownLocation(LocationManager.GPS_PR
OVIDER);
    int lat, lng;
    if(location != null) {
        //Convert to microdegrees
        lat = (int)(location.getLatitude() * 1000000);
        lng = (int)(location.getLongitude() * 1000000);
    } else {
        //Default to Google HQ
        lat = 37427222;
        lng = -122099167;
    }
    GeoPoint mapCenter = new GeoPoint(lat,lng);
    controller.setCenter(mapCenter);
    controller.setZoom(15);
}
```

3. Code for Maps in Street View

```java
package app.test;
```

```
import android.os.Bundle;
import android.view.View;
import com.google.android.maps.MapActivity;
import com.google.android.maps.MapView;

import android.content.Context;
import android.content.Intent;
import android.net.Uri;
import android.util.Log;

import com.google.android.maps.GeoPoint;
import com.google.android.maps.MapView;
import com.google.android.maps.Overlay;

class ClickReceiver extends Overlay{
  private static final String TAG = "ClickReceiver";
  private Context mContext;

  public ClickReceiver(Context context) {
    mContext = context;
  }

  @Override
```

```
public boolean onTap(GeoPoint p, MapView mapView) {

  Log.v(TAG, "Received a click at this point: " + p);

  if(mapView.isStreetView()) {

      Intent myIntent = new Intent(Intent.ACTION_VIEW,
Uri.parse

      ("google.streetview:cbll=" +

      (float)p.getLatitudeE6() / 1000000f +

      "," + (float)p.getLongitudeE6() / 1000000f

       +"&cbp=1,180,,0,1.0"

        ));

    mContext.startActivity(myIntent);

    return true;

  }

   return false;

 }
}


public class MainActivity extends MapActivity
{

  private MapView mapView;


  @Override

  protected void onCreate(Bundle savedInstanceState) {
```

```
super.onCreate(savedInstanceState);
setContentView(R.layout.main);
mapView = (MapView)findViewById(R.id.mapview);
ClickReceiver clickRecvr = new ClickReceiver(this);
mapView.getOverlays().add(clickRecvr);
mapView.invalidate();
}


public void myClickHandler(View target) {
  switch(target.getId()) {
  case R.id.zoomin:
    mapView.getController().zoomIn();
    break;
  case R.id.zoomout:
    mapView.getController().zoomOut();
    break;
  case R.id.sat:
    mapView.setSatellite(true);
    break;
  case R.id.street:
    mapView.setStreetView(true);
    break;
  case R.id.traffic:
```

```
   mapView.setTraffic(true);
   break;
 case R.id.normal:
   mapView.setSatellite(false);
   mapView.setStreetView(false);
   mapView.setTraffic(false);
   break;
 }
 mapView.postInvalidateDelayed(2000);
}
@Override
protected boolean isLocationDisplayed() {
  return false;
}

@Override
protected boolean isRouteDisplayed() {
  return false;
}
}
```

//main.xml

```xml
<?xml version="1.0" encoding="utf-8"?>

  <!-- This file is /res/layout/mapview.xml -->
<LinearLayout
xmlns:android="http://schemas.android.com/apk/res/android"

  android:orientation="vertical"
android:layout_width="fill_parent"

  android:layout_height="fill_parent">


  <LinearLayout
xmlns:android="http://schemas.android.com/apk/res/android"

  android:orientation="horizontal"
android:layout_width="fill_parent"

  android:layout_height="wrap_content">


  <Button android:id="@+id/zoomin"
android:layout_width="wrap_content"

    android:layout_height="wrap_content" android:text="+"

    android:onClick="myClickHandler"
android:padding="12px" />


  <Button android:id="@+id/zoomout"
android:layout_width="wrap_content"

    android:layout_height="wrap_content" android:text="-"
```

```
      android:onClick="myClickHandler"
android:padding="12px" />


   <Button android:id="@+id/sat"
android:layout_width="wrap_content"

      android:layout_height="wrap_content"
android:text="Satellite"

      android:onClick="myClickHandler"
android:padding="8px" />


   <Button android:id="@+id/street"
android:layout_width="wrap_content"

      android:layout_height="wrap_content"
android:text="Street"

      android:onClick="myClickHandler"
android:padding="8px" />


   <Button android:id="@+id/traffic"
android:layout_width="wrap_content"

      android:layout_height="wrap_content"
android:text="Traffic"

      android:onClick="myClickHandler"
android:padding="8px" />


   <Button android:id="@+id/normal"
android:layout_width="wrap_content"
```

```
    android:layout_height="wrap_content"
android:text="Normal"

    android:onClick="myClickHandler"
android:padding="8px" />


  </LinearLayout>


  <com.google.android.maps.MapView

    android:id="@+id/mapview"
android:layout_width="fill_parent"

    android:layout_height="wrap_content"
android:clickable="true"

    android:apiKey="YourKey" />


</LinearLayout>
```

4. Code for Street View Maps with Pinch Zoom Feature

```
package app.test;


import android.os.Bundle;

import android.view.View;

import com.google.android.maps.MapActivity;

import com.google.android.maps.MapView;
```

```
import android.content.Context;

import android.content.Intent;

import android.net.Uri;

import android.util.FloatMath;

import android.util.Log;

import android.view.MotionEvent;

import com.google.android.maps.GeoPoint;

import com.google.android.maps.MapView;

import com.google.android.maps.Overlay;


class ClickReceiver extends Overlay {
  private static final float ZOOMJUMP = 75f;
  private Context mContext;
  private boolean inZoomMode = false;
  private boolean ignoreLastFinger = false;
  private float mOrigSeparation;

  public ClickReceiver(Context context) {
      mContext = context;
  }

  @Override
  public boolean onTap(GeoPoint p, MapView mapView) {
```

```
if(mapView.isStreetView()) {

        Intent myIntent = new Intent(Intent.ACTION_VIEW,
Uri.parse

        ("google.streetview:cbll=" +

        (float)p.getLatitudeE6() / 1000000f +

        "," + (float)p.getLongitudeE6() / 1000000f

         +"&cbp=1,180,,0,1.0"

          ));

     mContext.startActivity(myIntent);

     return true;

  }

    return false;

  }


  public boolean onTouchEvent(MotionEvent e, MapView
mapView) {

    int action = e.getAction() &
MotionEvent.ACTION_MASK;


    if(e.getPointerCount() == 2) {

      inZoomMode = true;

    }

    else {

      inZoomMode = false;
```

```
}


if(inZoomMode) {
  switch(action) {
  case MotionEvent.ACTION_POINTER_DOWN:
    mOrigSeparation = calculateSeparation(e);
    break;
  case MotionEvent.ACTION_POINTER_UP:
    ignoreLastFinger  = true;
    break;
  case MotionEvent.ACTION_MOVE:
    float newSeparation = calculateSeparation(e);
    if(newSeparation - mOrigSeparation > ZOOMJUMP) {
      mapView.getController().zoomIn();
      mOrigSeparation = newSeparation;
    }
    else if (mOrigSeparation - newSeparation >
ZOOMJUMP) {
      mapView.getController().zoomOut();
      mOrigSeparation = newSeparation;
    }
    break;
  }
```

```
      return true;
    }
    if(ignoreLastFinger) {
      if(action == MotionEvent.ACTION_UP)
        ignoreLastFinger = false;
      return true;
    }
  return super.onTouchEvent(e, mapView);
}
private float calculateSeparation(MotionEvent e) {
  float x = e.getX(0) - e.getX(1);
  float y = e.getY(0) - e.getY(1);
  return FloatMath.sqrt(x * x + y * y);
  }
}


public class MainActivity extends MapActivity
{
  private MapView mapView;

  @Override
  protected void onCreate(Bundle savedInstanceState) {
    super.onCreate(savedInstanceState);
```

```
    setContentView(R.layout.main);

    mapView = (MapView)findViewById(R.id.mapview);

    ClickReceiver clickRecvr = new ClickReceiver(this);
    mapView.getOverlays().add(clickRecvr);
    mapView.invalidate();
}

public void myClickHandler(View target) {
    switch(target.getId()) {
    case R.id.zoomin:
      mapView.getController().zoomIn();
      break;
    case R.id.zoomout:
      mapView.getController().zoomOut();
      break;
    case R.id.sat:
      mapView.setSatellite(true);
      break;
    case R.id.street:
      mapView.setStreetView(true);
      break;
```

```java
    case R.id.traffic:
      mapView.setTraffic(true);
      break;
    case R.id.normal:
      mapView.setSatellite(false);
      mapView.setStreetView(false);
      mapView.setTraffic(false);
      break;
    }
    mapView.postInvalidateDelayed(2000);
  }

  @Override
  protected boolean isLocationDisplayed() {
    return false;
  }

  @Override
  protected boolean isRouteDisplayed() {
    return false;
  }
}
<?xml version="1.0" encoding="utf-8"?>
```

```
<!-- This file is /res/layout/mapview.xml -->

<LinearLayout
xmlns:android="http://schemas.android.com/apk/res/andr
oid"

android:orientation="vertical"
android:layout_width="fill_parent"

android:layout_height="fill_parent">


<LinearLayout
xmlns:android="http://schemas.android.com/apk/res/andr
oid"

android:orientation="horizontal"
android:layout_width="fill_parent"

android:layout_height="wrap_content">


<Button android:id="@+id/zoomin"
android:layout_width="wrap_content"

 android:layout_height="wrap_content" android:text="+"

 android:onClick="myClickHandler"
android:padding="12px" />


<Button android:id="@+id/zoomout"
android:layout_width="wrap_content"

 android:layout_height="wrap_content" android:text="-"

 android:onClick="myClickHandler"
android:padding="12px" />
```

```
<Button android:id="@+id/sat"
android:layout_width="wrap_content"

  android:layout_height="wrap_content"
android:text="Satellite"

  android:onClick="myClickHandler"
android:padding="8px" />


<Button android:id="@+id/street"
android:layout_width="wrap_content"

  android:layout_height="wrap_content"
android:text="Street"

  android:onClick="myClickHandler"
android:padding="8px" />


<Button android:id="@+id/traffic"
android:layout_width="wrap_content"

  android:layout_height="wrap_content"
android:text="Traffic"

  android:onClick="myClickHandler"
android:padding="8px" />


<Button android:id="@+id/normal"
android:layout_width="wrap_content"

  android:layout_height="wrap_content"
android:text="Normal"
```

```
  android:onClick="myClickHandler"
android:padding="8px" />
```

```
</LinearLayout>
```

```
<com.google.android.maps.MapView
```

```
android:id="@+id/mapview"
android:layout_width="fill_parent"
```

```
android:layout_height="wrap_content"
android:clickable="true"
```

```
android:apiKey="YourKey" />
```

```
</LinearLayout>
```

5. Code for the Voice Recognition Feature

```
package app.test;
```

```
import java.util.ArrayList;
```

```
import android.app.Activity;
```

```
import android.app.AlertDialog;
```

```
import android.content.ActivityNotFoundException;
```

```
import android.content.DialogInterface;
```

```
import android.content.Intent;
```

```java
import android.net.Uri;

import android.os.Bundle;

import android.speech.RecognizerIntent;

import android.widget.TextView;

import android.widget.Toast;


public class Test extends Activity {
    private static final int REQUEST_RECOGNIZE = 100;
    TextView tv;
    @Override
    public void onCreate(Bundle savedInstanceState) {
        super.onCreate(savedInstanceState);
        tv = new TextView(this);
        setContentView(tv);


        Intent intent = new
Intent(RecognizerIntent.ACTION_RECOGNIZE_SPEECH);

intent.putExtra(RecognizerIntent.EXTRA_LANGUAGE_MODEL,
RecognizerIntent.LANGUAGE_MODEL_FREE_FORM);

        intent.putExtra(RecognizerIntent.EXTRA_PROMPT,
"Tell Me Your Name");
        try {
```

```
    startActivityForResult(intent,
REQUEST_RECOGNIZE);

  } catch (ActivityNotFoundException e) {

    AlertDialog.Builder builder = new
AlertDialog.Builder(this);

      builder.setTitle("Not Available");

      builder.setMessage("No recognition software
installed.Download one?");

      builder.setPositiveButton("Yes", new
DialogInterface.OnClickListener() {

        @Override

        public void onClick(DialogInterface dialog, int
which) {

          Intent marketIntent = new
Intent(Intent.ACTION_VIEW);

marketIntent.setData(Uri.parse("market://details?id=com.g
oogle.android.voicesearch"));

        }

      });

      builder.setNegativeButton("No", null);

      builder.create().show();

  }

}


  @Override
```

```
    protected void onActivityResult(int requestCode, int
resultCode, Intent data) {

    if(requestCode == REQUEST_RECOGNIZE &&
resultCode == Activity.RESULT_OK) {

        ArrayList<String> matches =
data.getStringArrayListExtra(RecognizerIntent.EXTRA_RE
SULTS);

        StringBuilder sb = new StringBuilder();

        for(String piece : matches) {

            sb.append(piece);

            sb.append('\n');

        }

        tv.setText(sb.toString());

    } else {

        Toast.makeText(this, "Operation Canceled",
Toast.LENGTH_SHORT).show();

    }

  }

}
```

6. Managing Your Contacts List

```
    package app.test;


    import android.app.ListActivity;

    import android.database.Cursor;
```

```java
import android.net.Uri;

import android.os.Bundle;

import android.provider.ContactsContract;

import android.util.Log;

import android.widget.SimpleCursorAdapter;


public class Test extends ListActivity {
  @Override
  public void onCreate(Bundle savedInstanceState) {
    super.onCreate(savedInstanceState);

    setContentView(R.layout.main);

    //Uri allContacts =
Uri.parse("content://contacts/people");

    //Uri allContacts =
Uri.parse("content://contacts/people/1");

    Uri allContacts =
ContactsContract.Contacts.CONTENT_URI;

    //Uri allContacts =
ContentUris.withAppendedId(ContactsContract.Contacts.CONTENT_URI, 1);

    String[] projection = new String[]
      {ContactsContract.Contacts._ID,

        ContactsContract.Contacts.DISPLAY_NAME,


ContactsContract.Contacts.HAS_PHONE_NUMBER};
```

```
Cursor c = managedQuery(
    allContacts,
    projection,
    ContactsContract.Contacts.DISPLAY_NAME + " LIKE
?",
    new String[] {"%"} ,
    ContactsContract.Contacts.DISPLAY_NAME + "
ASC");



String[] columns = new String[]
{ContactsContract.Contacts._ID,
ContactsContract.Contacts.DISPLAY_NAME,};
    int[] views = new int[] {R.id.contactName,
R.id.contactID};


SimpleCursorAdapter adapter =
    new SimpleCursorAdapter(this, R.layout.main, c,
columns, views);
    this.setListAdapter(adapter);


PrintContacts(c);
}
```

```
private void PrintContacts(Cursor c)

{

    if (c.moveToFirst()) {

        do{

            String contactID =
c.getString(c.getColumnIndex(ContactsContract.Contacts._I
D));

            String contactDisplayName =
c.getString(c.getColumnIndex(ContactsContract.Contacts.DI
SPLAY_NAME));

            Log.v("Content Providers", contactID + ", " +
contactDisplayName);

            int hasPhone =
c.getInt(c.getColumnIndex(ContactsContract.Contacts.HAS
_PHONE_NUMBER));

            if (hasPhone == 1) {

                Cursor phoneCursor =
getContentResolver().query(


ContactsContract.CommonDataKinds.Phone.CONTENT_UR
I, null,


ContactsContract.CommonDataKinds.Phone.CONTACT_ID
+ " = " + contactID, null, null);

                while (phoneCursor.moveToNext()) {

                    Log.v("Content Providers",
```

```
phoneCursor.getString(phoneCursor.getColumnIndex(Conta
ctsContract.CommonDataKinds.Phone.NUMBER)));
        }
        phoneCursor.close();
      }
    } while (c.moveToNext());
  }
  }
}
```

//main.xml

```xml
<?xml version="1.0" encoding="utf-8"?>
<LinearLayout
xmlns:android="http://schemas.android.com/apk/res/andr
oid"
  android:orientation="vertical"
  android:layout_width="fill_parent"
  android:layout_height="fill_parent"
  >
  <ListView
    android:id="@+id/android:list"
```

```
    android:layout_width="fill_parent"
    android:layout_height="wrap_content"
    android:layout_weight="1"
    android:stackFromBottom="false"
    android:transcriptMode="normal"
    />
<TextView
    android:id="@+id/contactName"
    android:textStyle="bold"
    android:layout_width="wrap_content"
    android:layout_height="wrap_content"
    />
<TextView
    android:id="@+id/contactID"
    android:layout_width="fill_parent"
    android:layout_height="wrap_content"
    />

</LinearLayout>
```

7. Setting up the Alarm

```
<?xml version="1.0" encoding="utf-8"?>
```

```xml
<LinearLayout
xmlns:android="http://schemas.android.com/apk/res/android"
  android:orientation="vertical"
  android:layout_width="fill_parent"
  android:layout_height="fill_parent">
  <Button
   android:id="@+id/start"
   android:layout_width="fill_parent"
   android:layout_height="wrap_content"
   android:text="Start Alarm"
 />
  <Button
   android:id="@+id/stop"
   android:layout_width="fill_parent"
   android:layout_height="wrap_content"
   android:text="Cancel Alarm"
 />
</LinearLayout>
```

```java
package app.test;

import java.util.Calendar;

import android.app.Activity;
```

```java
import android.app.AlarmManager;

import android.app.PendingIntent;

import android.content.Context;

import android.content.Intent;

import android.os.Bundle;

import android.os.SystemClock;

import android.view.View;

import android.widget.Toast;


public class AlarmActivity extends Activity implements
View.OnClickListener {

    private PendingIntent mAlarmIntent;

    @Override
    public void onCreate(Bundle savedInstanceState) {
        super.onCreate(savedInstanceState);
        setContentView(R.layout.main);
        findViewById(R.id.start).setOnClickListener(this);
        findViewById(R.id.stop).setOnClickListener(this);
        Intent launchIntent = new Intent(this,
AlarmReceiver.class);
        mAlarmIntent = PendingIntent.getBroadcast(this, 0,
launchIntent, 0);
```

```
    }


    @Override

    public void onClick(View v) {

    AlarmManager manager =
(AlarmManager)getSystemService(Context.ALARM_SERVI
CE);

    long interval = 5*1000; //5 seconds


    switch(v.getId()) {

    case R.id.start:

        Toast.makeText(this, "Scheduled",
Toast.LENGTH_SHORT).show();


manager.setRepeating(AlarmManager.ELAPSED_REALTIM
E,

            SystemClock.elapsedRealtime()+interval,

            interval,

            mAlarmIntent);

        break;

    case R.id.stop:

        Toast.makeText(this, "Canceled",
Toast.LENGTH_SHORT).show();

            manager.cancel(mAlarmIntent);

            break;
```

```java
      default:
        break;
    }
  }


  private long nextStartTime() {
    long oneDay = 24*3600*1000; //24 hours
    //Set the time to 09:00:00
    Calendar startTime = Calendar.getInstance();
    startTime.set(Calendar.HOUR_OF_DAY, 9);
    startTime.set(Calendar.MINUTE, 0);
    startTime.set(Calendar.SECOND, 0);

    Calendar now = Calendar.getInstance();
    if(now.before(startTime)) {
      return startTime.getTimeInMillis();
    } else {
      startTime.add(Calendar.DATE, 1);
      return startTime.getTimeInMillis();
    }
  }
}
```

```
package app.test;

import java.text.DateFormat;
import java.text.SimpleDateFormat;
import java.util.Calendar;

import android.content.BroadcastReceiver;
import android.content.Context;
import android.content.Intent;
import android.widget.Toast;

public class AlarmReceiver extends BroadcastReceiver {
    @Override
    public void onReceive(Context context, Intent intent) {
        Calendar now = Calendar.getInstance();
        DateFormat formatter =
SimpleDateFormat.getTimeInstance();
        Toast.makeText(context,
formatter.format(now.getTime()),
Toast.LENGTH_SHORT).show();
    }
}
```

8. Setting up one-shot alarms and repeated alarms

```
/*
 * Copyright (C) 2007 The Android Open Source Project
 *
 * Licensed under the Apache License, Version 2.0 (the
"License");
 * you may not use this file except in compliance with the
License.
 * You may obtain a copy of the License at
 *
 *    http://www.apache.org/licenses/LICENSE-2.0
 *
 * Unless required by applicable law or agreed to in writing,
software
 * distributed under the License is distributed on an "AS IS"
BASIS,
 * WITHOUT WARRANTIES OR CONDITIONS OF ANY
KIND, either express or implied.
 * See the License for the specific language governing
permissions and
 * limitations under the License.
 */


package app.test;
```

```java
import java.util.Calendar;

import android.app.Activity;
import android.app.AlarmManager;
import android.app.PendingIntent;
import android.content.BroadcastReceiver;
import android.content.Context;
import android.content.Intent;
import android.os.Bundle;
import android.os.SystemClock;
import android.view.View;
import android.view.View.OnClickListener;
import android.widget.Button;
import android.widget.Toast;

/**
 * Example of scheduling one-shot and repeating alarms. See
{@link OneShotAlarm}
 * for the code run when the one-shot alarm goes off, and
{@link RepeatingAlarm}
 * for the code run when the repeating alarm goes off.
<h4>Demo</h4>
 * App/Service/Alarm Controller
 *
```

* <h4>Source files</h4>

* <table class="LinkTable">

* <tr>

* <td class="LinkColumn">src/com.example.android.apis/app/Test.java</td>

* <td class="DescrColumn">The activity that lets you schedule alarms</td>

* </tr>

* <tr>

* <td class="LinkColumn">src/com.example.android.apis/app/OneShotAlarm.java</td>

* <td class="DescrColumn">This is an intent receiver that executes when the

* one-shot alarm goes off</td>

* </tr>

* <tr>

* <td class="LinkColumn">src/com.example.android.apis/app/RepeatingAlarm.java</td>

* <td class="DescrColumn">This is an intent receiver that executes when the

* repeating alarm goes off</td>

* </tr>

* <tr>

```
 * <td
class="LinkColumn">/res/any/layout/alarm_controller.xml
</td>
 * <td class="DescrColumn">Defines contents of the
screen</td>
 * </tr>
 * </table>
 */
public class Test extends Activity {
  Toast mToast;

  @Override
  protected void onCreate(Bundle savedInstanceState) {
    super.onCreate(savedInstanceState);

    setContentView(R.layout.main);

    // Watch for button clicks.
    Button button = (Button) findViewById(R.id.one_shot);
    button.setOnClickListener(mOneShotListener);
    button = (Button) findViewById(R.id.start_repeating);
    button.setOnClickListener(mStartRepeatingListener);
    button = (Button) findViewById(R.id.stop_repeating);
    button.setOnClickListener(mStopRepeatingListener);
```

```
}


  private OnClickListener mOneShotListener = new
OnClickListener() {

  public void onClick(View v) {

    // When the alarm goes off, we want to broadcast an
Intent to our

    // BroadcastReceiver. Here we make an Intent with an
explicit class

    // name to have our own receiver (which has been
published in

    // AndroidManifest.xml) instantiated and called, and
then create an

    // IntentSender to have the intent executed as a
broadcast.

    Intent intent = new Intent(Test.this,
OneShotAlarm.class);

    PendingIntent sender =
PendingIntent.getBroadcast(Test.this, 0,

       intent, 0);


    // We want the alarm to go off 30 seconds from now.

    Calendar calendar = Calendar.getInstance();

    calendar.setTimeInMillis(System.currentTimeMillis());

    calendar.add(Calendar.SECOND, 30);
```

```
// Schedule the alarm!

AlarmManager am = (AlarmManager)
getSystemService(ALARM_SERVICE);

am.set(AlarmManager.RTC_WAKEUP,
calendar.getTimeInMillis(), sender);


// Tell the user about what we did.

if (mToast != null) {

  mToast.cancel();

}

mToast = Toast.makeText(Test.this,
"one_shot_scheduled",

    Toast.LENGTH_LONG);

mToast.show();

 }

};


 private OnClickListener mStartRepeatingListener = new
OnClickListener() {

 public void onClick(View v) {

// When the alarm goes off, we want to broadcast an
Intent to our

// BroadcastReceiver. Here we make an Intent with an
explicit class
```

// name to have our own receiver (which has been published in

// AndroidManifest.xml) instantiated and called, and then create an

// IntentSender to have the intent executed as a broadcast.

// Note that unlike above, this IntentSender is configured to

// allow itself to be sent multiple times.

```
Intent intent = new Intent(Test.this,
RepeatingAlarm.class);

PendingIntent sender =
PendingIntent.getBroadcast(Test.this, 0,

    intent, 0);
```

// We want the alarm to go off 30 seconds from now.

```
long firstTime = SystemClock.elapsedRealtime();

firstTime += 15 * 1000;
```

// Schedule the alarm!

```
AlarmManager am = (AlarmManager)
getSystemService(ALARM_SERVICE);

am.setRepeating(AlarmManager.ELAPSED_REALTIME_W
AKEUP, firstTime,

    15 * 1000, sender);
```

```
// Tell the user about what we did.
if (mToast != null) {
  mToast.cancel();
}
mToast = Toast.makeText(Test.this,
"repeating_scheduled",
    Toast.LENGTH_LONG);
  mToast.show();
 }
};
```

```
private OnClickListener mStopRepeatingListener = new
OnClickListener() {
  public void onClick(View v) {
   // Create the same intent, and thus a matching
IntentSender, for
   // the one that was scheduled.
   Intent intent = new Intent(Test.this,
RepeatingAlarm.class);
   PendingIntent sender =
PendingIntent.getBroadcast(Test.this, 0,
     intent, 0);
```

```
   // And cancel the alarm.
```

```
    AlarmManager am = (AlarmManager)
getSystemService(ALARM_SERVICE);

    am.cancel(sender);


    // Tell the user about what we did.

    if (mToast != null) {

      mToast.cancel();

    }

    mToast = Toast.makeText(Test.this,
"repeating_unscheduled",

        Toast.LENGTH_LONG);

    mToast.show();

  }

 };

}


/**

 * This is an example of implement an {@link
BroadcastReceiver} for an alarm that

 * should occur once.

 * <p>

 * When the alarm goes off, we show a <i>Toast</i>, a quick
message.

 */
```

```
class OneShotAlarm extends BroadcastReceiver
{
    @Override
    public void onReceive(Context context, Intent intent)
    {
        Toast.makeText(context, "one_shot_received",
Toast.LENGTH_SHORT).show();
    }
}



/**
 * This is an example of implement an {@link
BroadcastReceiver} for an alarm
 * that should occur once.
 */
class RepeatingAlarm extends BroadcastReceiver {
    @Override
    public void onReceive(Context context, Intent intent) {
        Toast.makeText(context, "repeating_received",
Toast.LENGTH_SHORT)
            .show();
    }
}
```

//main.xml

<?xml version="1.0" encoding="utf-8"?>

<!-- Copyright (C) 2007 The Android Open Source Project

Licensed under the Apache License, Version 2.0 (the "License");

you may not use this file except in compliance with the License.

You may obtain a copy of the License at

http://www.apache.org/licenses/LICENSE-2.0

Unless required by applicable law or agreed to in writing, software

distributed under the License is distributed on an "AS IS" BASIS,

WITHOUT WARRANTIES OR CONDITIONS OF ANY KIND, either express or implied.

See the License for the specific language governing permissions and

limitations under the License.

-->

<!-- Demonstrates starting and stopping a local service.

See corresponding Java code
com.android.sdk.app.LocalSerice.java. -->

```xml
<LinearLayout
xmlns:android="http://schemas.android.com/apk/res/android" android:orientation="vertical" android:padding="4dip"

    android:gravity="center_horizontal"

    android:layout_width="match_parent"
android:layout_height="match_parent">


    <TextView

    android:layout_width="match_parent"
android:layout_height="wrap_content"

    android:layout_weight="0"

    android:paddingBottom="4dip"

    android:text="alarm_controller"/>


    <Button android:id="@+id/one_shot"

    android:layout_width="wrap_content"
android:layout_height="wrap_content"

    android:text="one_shot_alarm">

    <requestFocus />

    </Button>


    <Button android:id="@+id/start_repeating"
```

```
android:layout_width="wrap_content"
android:layout_height="wrap_content"

    android:text="start_repeating_alarm" />


  <Button android:id="@+id/stop_repeating"

    android:layout_width="wrap_content"
android:layout_height="wrap_content"

    android:text="stop_repeating_alarm" />
```

```
</LinearLayout>
```

b. Authentication Codes

1. Code for web authentication

```
//package com.maxiujun.android.doudroid.test.utils;


import java.io.BufferedReader;

import java.io.IOException;

import java.io.InputStream;

import java.io.InputStreamReader;

import java.io.UnsupportedEncodingException;

import java.net.URLEncoder;

import java.util.regex.Matcher;

import java.util.regex.Pattern;


import org.apache.http.HttpResponse;
```

```
import org.apache.http.client.ClientProtocolException;

import org.apache.http.client.HttpClient;

import org.apache.http.client.methods.HttpGet;

import org.apache.http.client.methods.HttpPost;

import org.apache.http.client.params.ClientPNames;

import org.apache.http.client.params.CookiePolicy;

import org.apache.http.conn.ClientConnectionManager;

import org.apache.http.conn.scheme.PlainSocketFactory;

import org.apache.http.conn.scheme.Scheme;

import org.apache.http.conn.scheme.SchemeRegistry;

import org.apache.http.conn.ssl.SSLSocketFactory;

import org.apache.http.entity.StringEntity;

import org.apache.http.impl.client.DefaultHttpClient;

import
org.apache.http.impl.conn.tsccm.ThreadSafeClientConnM
anager;


/**
 * Type comments here.
 *
 * @author Xiujun Ma <maxj@adv.emcom.jp>
 * @version Jul 31, 2010
 */
class OauthWebConfirm {
```

```
private static HttpClient httpClient = new CHttpClient();

public static String email = "";

public static String pwd = "";


public static void confirm(String url) {

httpClient.getParams().setParameter(ClientPNames.COO
KIE_POLICY,
CookiePolicy.BROWSER_COMPATIBILITY);

    try {


    // login

    HttpPost loginpost = new
HttpPost("http://www.douban.com/login");


    String loginentity = "redir=&form_email=" +
URLEncoder.encode(email, "UTF-8") +
"&form_password=" + URLEncoder.encode(pwd, "UTF-
8")
+"&remember=on&user_login=%E8%BF%9B%E5%85%A
5";


    StringEntity reqEntity = new StringEntity(loginentity);

    reqEntity.setContentType("application/x-www-form-
urlencoded");

    loginpost.setEntity(reqEntity);
```

loginpost.setHeader("User-Agent", "Mozilla/5.0 (Windows; U; Windows NT 5.1; zh-CN; rv:1.9.2.8) Gecko/20100722 Firefox/3.6.8");

httpClient.execute(loginpost);

// agree page

HttpGet get = new HttpGet(url);

get.setHeader("User-Agent", "Mozilla/5.0 (Windows; U; Windows NT 5.1; zh-CN; rv:1.9.2.8) Gecko/20100722 Firefox/3.6.8");

HttpResponse res2 = httpClient.execute(get);

String restring2 = convertStreamToString(res2.getEntity().getContent());

// agree action

HttpPost agreepost = new HttpPost(url);

StringBuilder stringBuilder = new StringBuilder();

stringBuilder.append("oauth_token=").append(getFromValue(restring2, "oauth_token"));

stringBuilder.append("&oauth_callback=").append(getFromValue(restring2, "oauth_callback"));

```
stringBuilder.append("&ssid=").append(getFromValue(re
string2, "ssid"));

stringBuilder.append("&confirm=").append(getFromValu
e(restring2, "confirm"));


    StringEntity agreeEntity = new
StringEntity(stringBuilder.toString());
    agreeEntity.setContentType("application/x-www-
form-urlencoded");
    agreepost.setEntity(agreeEntity);
    agreepost.setHeader("User-Agent", "Mozilla/5.0
(Windows; U; Windows NT 5.1; zh-CN; rv:1.9.2.8)
Gecko/20100722 Firefox/3.6.8");
    httpClient.execute(agreepost);
    // HttpResponse res3 = httpClient.execute(agreepost);


    // String restring3 =
convertStreamToString(res3.getEntity().getContent());

} catch (ClientProtocolException e) {
  e.printStackTrace();
} catch (IOException e) {
  e.printStackTrace();
}
```

```
}


  public static String convertStreamToString(InputStream
is) throws IOException {
    if (is != null) {
    StringBuilder sb = new StringBuilder();
    String line;


    try {
      BufferedReader reader = new BufferedReader(new
InputStreamReader(is, "UTF-8"));
      while ((line = reader.readLine()) != null) {
        sb.append(line).append("\n");
      }
    } finally {
      is.close();
    }
    return sb.toString();
    } else {
    return "";
    }
  }
```

```java
 public static String getFromValue(String html, String name) {


    Pattern p = Pattern.compile("name=\\\"" + name + "\\\" value=\\\".+\\\"");
    Matcher m = p.matcher(html);
    String ex = "";
    if(m.find()) ex = m.group(0);
    else return "";
    String value = "";
       try {
       value = URLEncoder.encode(ex.split("value=\"")[1].replace("\"", ""), "UTF-8");
       } catch (UnsupportedEncodingException e) {
        e.printStackTrace();
       }
    return value;
  }
}




class CHttpClient extends DefaultHttpClient {
```

```
@Override

 protected ClientConnectionManager
createClientConnectionManager() {

  SchemeRegistry registry = new SchemeRegistry();

  registry.register(new Scheme("http",
PlainSocketFactory.getSocketFactory(), 80));

  registry.register(new Scheme("https",
SSLSocketFactory.getSocketFactory(), 443));


  return new
ThreadSafeClientConnManager(this.getParams(),
registry);

 }

}
```

c. Code for Dates

1. Coding the elapsed time

```
/*

 * AFreeChart : a free chart library for Android(tm)
platform.

 *        (based on JFreeChart and JCommon)

 *

 *

 * (C) Copyright 2010, by Icom Systech Co., Ltd.

 * (C) Copyright 2000-2008, by Object Refinery
Limited and Contributors.
```

*

* Project Info:

*   AFreeChart: http://code.google.com/p/afreechart/

*   JFreeChart:
http://www.jfree.org/jfreechart/index.html

*   JCommon   :
http://www.jfree.org/jcommon/index.html

*

* This program is free software: you can redistribute it and/or modify

* it under the terms of the GNU General Public License as published by

* the Free Software Foundation, either version 3 of the License, or

* (at your option) any later version.

*

* This program is distributed in the hope that it will be useful,

* but WITHOUT ANY WARRANTY; without even the implied warranty of

* MERCHANTABILITY or FITNESS FOR A PARTICULAR PURPOSE. See the

* GNU General Public License for more details.

*

* You should have received a copy of the GNU General Public License

* along with this program. If not, see
<http://www.gnu.org/licenses/>.

*

* [Android is a trademark of Google Inc.]

*

* -----------------------

* RelativeDateFormat.java

* -----------------------

*

* (C) Copyright 2010, by Icom Systech Co., Ltd.

*

* Original Author: shiraki (for Icom Systech Co., Ltd);

* Contributor(s):   Sato Yoshiaki ;

*   Niwano Masayoshi;

*

* Changes (from 19-Nov-2010)

* --------------------------

* 19-Nov-2010 : port JFreeChart 1.0.13 to Android as
"AFreeChart"

*

* ------------- JFreeChart ------------------------------------
----

* (C) Copyright 2006-2008, by Object Refinery Limited
and Contributors.

```
*

* Original Author:  David Gilbert (for Object Refinery
Limited);

* Contributor(s):  Michael Siemer;

*

* Changes:

* --------

* 01-Nov-2006 : Version 1 (DG);

* 23-Nov-2006 : Added argument checks, updated
equals(), added clone() and

*           hashCode() (DG);

* 15-Feb-2008 : Applied patch 1873328 by Michael
Siemer, with minor

*           modifications (DG);

* 01-Sep-2008 : Added new fields for hour and minute
formatting, based on

*           patch 2033092 (DG);

*

*/


import java.text.DateFormat;

import java.text.DecimalFormat;

import java.text.FieldPosition;

import java.text.NumberFormat;
```

```
import java.text.ParsePosition;

import java.util.Calendar;

import java.util.Date;

import java.util.GregorianCalendar;


/**

 * A formatter that formats dates to show the elapsed
time relative to some

 * base date.

 *

 * @since JFreeChart 1.0.3

 */

public class RelativeDateFormat extends DateFormat {


    /**

     *

     */

    private static final long serialVersionUID = -
1923563381548016970L;


    /** The base milliseconds for the elapsed time
calculation. */

    private long baseMillis;
```

```
/**

    * A flag that controls whether or not a zero day count
is displayed.

    */

    private boolean showZeroDays;


/**

    * A flag that controls whether or not a zero hour
count is displayed.

    *

    * @since JFreeChart 1.0.10

    */

    private boolean showZeroHours;


/**

    * A formatter for the day count (most likely not
critical until the

    * day count exceeds 999).

    */

    private NumberFormat dayFormatter;


/**

    * A prefix prepended to the start of the format if the
relative date is
```

```
 * positive.
 *
 * @since JFreeChart 1.0.10
 */
private String positivePrefix;


/**
 * A string appended after the day count.
 */
private String daySuffix;


/**
 * A formatter for the hours.
 *
 * @since JFreeChart 1.0.11
 */
private NumberFormat hourFormatter;


/**
 * A string appended after the hours.
 */
private String hourSuffix;
```

```
/**
 * A formatter for the minutes.
 *
 * @since JFreeChart 1.0.11
 */
private NumberFormat minuteFormatter;

/**
 * A string appended after the minutes.
 */
private String minuteSuffix;

/**
 * A formatter for the seconds (and milliseconds).
 */
private NumberFormat secondFormatter;

/**
 * A string appended after the seconds.
 */
private String secondSuffix;

/**
```

```
     * A constant for the number of milliseconds in one
hour.
     */
     private static long
MILLISECONDS_IN_ONE_HOUR = 60 * 60 * 1000L;


    /**
     * A constant for the number of milliseconds in one
day.
     */
     private static long MILLISECONDS_IN_ONE_DAY
= 24 * MILLISECONDS_IN_ONE_HOUR;


    /**
     * Creates a new instance with base milliseconds set
to zero.
     */
     public RelativeDateFormat() {
        this(0L);
     }


    /**
     * Creates a new instance.
     *
```

```
   * @param time  the date/time (<code>null</code>
not permitted).
   */
  public RelativeDateFormat(Date time) {
    this(time.getTime());
  }


  /**
   * Creates a new instance.
   *
   * @param baseMillis  the time zone
(<code>null</code> not permitted).
   */
  public RelativeDateFormat(long baseMillis) {
    super();
    this.baseMillis = baseMillis;
    this.showZeroDays = false;
    this.showZeroHours = true;
    this.positivePrefix = "";
    this.dayFormatter =
NumberFormat.getNumberInstance();
    this.daySuffix = "d";
    this.hourFormatter =
NumberFormat.getNumberInstance();
```

```
    this.hourSuffix = "h";

    this.minuteFormatter =
NumberFormat.getNumberInstance();

    this.minuteSuffix = "m";

    this.secondFormatter =
NumberFormat.getNumberInstance();


this.secondFormatter.setMaximumFractionDigits(3);


this.secondFormatter.setMinimumFractionDigits(3);

    this.secondSuffix = "s";


    // we don't use the calendar or numberFormat
fields, but equals(Object)

    // is failing without them being non-null

    this.calendar = new GregorianCalendar();

    this.numberFormat = new DecimalFormat("0");
  }


  /**

   * Returns the base date/time used to calculate the
elapsed time for

   * display.

   *
```

```
 * @return The base date/time in milliseconds since
1-Jan-1970.

 *

 * @see #setBaseMillis(long)

 */
public long getBaseMillis() {

    return this.baseMillis;

}


/**

 * Sets the base date/time used to calculate the
elapsed time for display.

 * This should be specified in milliseconds using the
same encoding as

 * <code>java.util.Date</code>.

 *

 * @param baseMillis  the base date/time in
milliseconds.

 *

 * @see #getBaseMillis()

 */
public void setBaseMillis(long baseMillis) {

    this.baseMillis = baseMillis;

}
```

```
/**
 * Returns the flag that controls whether or not zero
day counts are
 * shown in the formatted output.
 *
 * @return The flag.
 *
 * @see #setShowZeroDays(boolean)
 */
public boolean getShowZeroDays() {
    return this.showZeroDays;
}


/**
 * Sets the flag that controls whether or not zero day
counts are shown
 * in the formatted output.
 *
 * @param show  the flag.
 *
 * @see #getShowZeroDays()
 */
public void setShowZeroDays(boolean show) {
```

```
      this.showZeroDays = show;
   }
```

```
   /**
    * Returns the flag that controls whether or not zero
hour counts are
    * shown in the formatted output.
    *
    * @return The flag.
    *
    * @see #setShowZeroHours(boolean)
    *
    * @since JFreeChart 1.0.10
    */
   public boolean getShowZeroHours() {
      return this.showZeroHours;
   }
```

```
   /**
    * Sets the flag that controls whether or not zero hour
counts are shown
    * in the formatted output.
    *
    * @param show  the flag.
```

```
*

* @see #getShowZeroHours()

*

* @since JFreeChart 1.0.10

*/
public void setShowZeroHours(boolean show) {

    this.showZeroHours = show;

}


/**

    * Returns the string that is prepended to the format
if the relative time

    * is positive.

    *

    * @return The string (never <code>null</code>).

    *

    * @see #setPositivePrefix(String)

    *

    * @since JFreeChart 1.0.10

    */
public String getPositivePrefix() {

    return this.positivePrefix;

}
```

```
/**
 * Sets the string that is prepended to the format if the
relative time is
 * positive.
 *
 * @param prefix  the prefix (<code>null</code> not
permitted).
 *
 * @see #getPositivePrefix()
 *
 * @since JFreeChart 1.0.10
 */
public void setPositivePrefix(String prefix) {
    if (prefix == null) {
        throw new IllegalArgumentException("Null
'prefix' argument.");
    }
    this.positivePrefix = prefix;
}


/**
 * Sets the formatter for the days.
 *
```

```
    * @param formatter  the formatter
(<code>null</code> not permitted).

    *

    * @since JFreeChart 1.0.11

    */

    public void setDayFormatter(NumberFormat
formatter) {

        if (formatter == null) {

            throw new IllegalArgumentException("Null
'formatter' argument.");

        }

        this.dayFormatter = formatter;

    }


    /**

    * Returns the string that is appended to the day
count.

    *

    * @return The string.

    *

    * @see #setDaySuffix(String)

    */

    public String getDaySuffix() {

        return this.daySuffix;
```

```
}


/**
 * Sets the string that is appended to the day count.
 *
 * @param suffix  the suffix (<code>null</code> not
permitted).
 *
 * @see #getDaySuffix()
 */
public void setDaySuffix(String suffix) {
    if (suffix == null) {
        throw new IllegalArgumentException("Null
'suffix' argument.");
    }
    this.daySuffix = suffix;
}


/**
 * Sets the formatter for the hours.
 *
 * @param formatter  the formatter
(<code>null</code> not permitted).
 *
```

```
  * @since JFreeChart 1.0.11
  */
  public void setHourFormatter(NumberFormat
formatter) {
      if (formatter == null) {
          throw new IllegalArgumentException("Null
'formatter' argument.");
      }
      this.hourFormatter = formatter;
  }


  /**
  * Returns the string that is appended to the hour
count.
  *
  * @return The string.
  *
  * @see #setHourSuffix(String)
  */
  public String getHourSuffix() {
      return this.hourSuffix;
  }


  /**
```

* Sets the string that is appended to the hour count.

*

* @param suffix the suffix (<code>null</code> not permitted).

*

* @see #getHourSuffix()

*/

```
public void setHourSuffix(String suffix) {
    if (suffix == null) {
        throw new IllegalArgumentException("Null
'suffix' argument.");
    }
    this.hourSuffix = suffix;
}
```

/**

* Sets the formatter for the minutes.

*

* @param formatter the formatter (<code>null</code> not permitted).

*

* @since JFreeChart 1.0.11

*/

```
    public void setMinuteFormatter(NumberFormat
formatter) {

        if (formatter == null) {

            throw new IllegalArgumentException("Null
'formatter' argument.");
        }

        this.minuteFormatter = formatter;
    }


    /**
     * Returns the string that is appended to the minute
count.
     *
     * @return The string.
     *
     * @see #setMinuteSuffix(String)
     */
    public String getMinuteSuffix() {

        return this.minuteSuffix;
    }


    /**
     * Sets the string that is appended to the minute
count.
```

```
     *

   * @param suffix  the suffix (<code>null</code> not
permitted).

     *

   * @see #getMinuteSuffix()

   */
   public void setMinuteSuffix(String suffix) {

      if (suffix == null) {

         throw new IllegalArgumentException("Null
'suffix' argument.");

      }

      this.minuteSuffix = suffix;

   }


   /**

   * Returns the string that is appended to the second
count.

     *

   * @return The string.

     *

   * @see #setSecondSuffix(String)

   */
   public String getSecondSuffix() {

      return this.secondSuffix;
```

```
    }


    /**

     * Sets the string that is appended to the second
count.

     *

     * @param suffix  the suffix (<code>null</code> not
permitted).

     *

     * @see #getSecondSuffix()

     */

    public void setSecondSuffix(String suffix) {

        if (suffix == null) {

            throw new IllegalArgumentException("Null
'suffix' argument.");

        }

        this.secondSuffix = suffix;

    }


    /**

     * Sets the formatter for the seconds and
milliseconds.

     *

     * @param formatter  the formatter
(<code>null</code> not permitted).
```

```
*/

public void setSecondFormatter(NumberFormat
formatter) {

    if (formatter == null) {

        throw new IllegalArgumentException("Null
'formatter' argument.");

    }

    this.secondFormatter = formatter;

}


/**
 * Formats the given date as the amount of elapsed
time (relative to the
 * base date specified in the constructor).
 *
 * @param date  the date.
 * @param toAppendTo  the string buffer.
 * @param fieldPosition  the field position.
 *
 * @return The formatted date.
 */
public StringBuffer format(Date date, StringBuffer
toAppendTo,

                FieldPosition fieldPosition) {
```

```
long currentMillis = date.getTime();

long elapsed = currentMillis - this.baseMillis;

String signPrefix;

if (elapsed < 0) {

    elapsed *= -1L;

    signPrefix = "-";

}

else {

    signPrefix = this.positivePrefix;

}


long days = elapsed /
MILLISECONDS_IN_ONE_DAY;

elapsed = elapsed - (days *
MILLISECONDS_IN_ONE_DAY);

long hours = elapsed /
MILLISECONDS_IN_ONE_HOUR;

elapsed = elapsed - (hours *
MILLISECONDS_IN_ONE_HOUR);

long minutes = elapsed / 60000L;

elapsed = elapsed - (minutes * 60000L);

double seconds = elapsed / 1000.0;


toAppendTo.append(signPrefix);
```

```
if (days != 0 || this.showZeroDays) {

toAppendTo.append(this.dayFormatter.format(days) +
getDaySuffix());
    }
    if (hours != 0 || this.showZeroHours) {

toAppendTo.append(this.hourFormatter.format(hours)
        + getHourSuffix());
    }

toAppendTo.append(this.minuteFormatter.format(min
utes)
        + getMinuteSuffix());

toAppendTo.append(this.secondFormatter.format(seco
nds)
        + getSecondSuffix());
    return toAppendTo;
  }


  /**
   * Parses the given string (not implemented).
   *
   * @param source  the date string.
```

```
 * @param pos  the parse position.
 *
 * @return <code>null</code>, as this method has
not been implemented.
 */
public Date parse(String source, ParsePosition pos) {
    return null;
}


/**
 * Tests this formatter for equality with an arbitrary
object.
 *
 * @param obj  the object (<code>null</code>
permitted).
 *
 * @return A boolean.
 */
public boolean equals(Object obj) {
    if (obj == this) {
        return true;
    }
    if (!(obj instanceof RelativeDateFormat)) {
        return false;
    }
```

```
    }
    if (!super.equals(obj)) {
        return false;
    }
    RelativeDateFormat that = (RelativeDateFormat)
obj;
    if (this.baseMillis != that.baseMillis) {
        return false;
    }
    if (this.showZeroDays != that.showZeroDays) {
        return false;
    }
    if (this.showZeroHours != that.showZeroHours) {
        return false;
    }
    if (!this.positivePrefix.equals(that.positivePrefix)) {
        return false;
    }
    if (!this.daySuffix.equals(that.daySuffix)) {
        return false;
    }
    if (!this.hourSuffix.equals(that.hourSuffix)) {
        return false;
```

```
    }
    if (!this.minuteSuffix.equals(that.minuteSuffix)) {
        return false;
    }
    if (!this.secondSuffix.equals(that.secondSuffix)) {
        return false;
    }
    if (!this.dayFormatter.equals(that.dayFormatter)) {
        return false;
    }
    if
(!this.hourFormatter.equals(that.hourFormatter)) {
        return false;
    }
    if
(!this.minuteFormatter.equals(that.minuteFormatter))
{
        return false;
    }
    if
(!this.secondFormatter.equals(that.secondFormatter))
{
        return false;
    }
    return true;
```

```
}


/**

 * Returns a hash code for this instance.

 *

 * @return A hash code.

 */
public int hashCode() {

    int result = 193;

    result = 37 * result

            + (int) (this.baseMillis ^ (this.baseMillis >>>
32));

    result = 37 * result +
this.positivePrefix.hashCode();

    result = 37 * result + this.daySuffix.hashCode();

    result = 37 * result + this.hourSuffix.hashCode();

    result = 37 * result + this.minuteSuffix.hashCode();

    result = 37 * result + this.secondSuffix.hashCode();

    result = 37 * result +
this.secondFormatter.hashCode();

    return result;

}


/**
```

```
     * Returns a clone of this instance.
     *
     * @return A clone.
     */
    public Object clone() {

        RelativeDateFormat clone = (RelativeDateFormat)
super.clone();

        clone.dayFormatter = (NumberFormat)
this.dayFormatter.clone();

        clone.secondFormatter = (NumberFormat)
this.secondFormatter.clone();

        return clone;

    }


    /**
     * Some test code.
     *
     * @param args  ignored.
     */
    public static void main(String[] args) {

    GregorianCalendar c0 = new
GregorianCalendar(2006, 10, 1, 0, 0, 0);

    GregorianCalendar c1 = new
GregorianCalendar(2006, 10, 1, 11, 37, 43);

        c1.set(Calendar.MILLISECOND, 123);
```

```
System.out.println("Default: ");
RelativeDateFormat rdf = new
RelativeDateFormat(co.getTime().getTime());
System.out.println(rdf.format(c1.getTime()));
System.out.println();


System.out.println("Hide milliseconds: ");
rdf.setSecondFormatter(new DecimalFormat("0"));
System.out.println(rdf.format(c1.getTime()));
System.out.println();


System.out.println("Show zero day output: ");
rdf.setShowZeroDays(true);
System.out.println(rdf.format(c1.getTime()));
System.out.println();


System.out.println("Alternative suffixes: ");
rdf.setShowZeroDays(false);
rdf.setDaySuffix(":");
rdf.setHourSuffix(":");
rdf.setMinuteSuffix(":");
rdf.setSecondSuffix("");
```

```
System.out.println(rdf.format(c1.getTime()));

System.out.println();

  }

}
```

2. Dates with timestamp

```
import java.text.SimpleDateFormat;

import java.util.Calendar;

import java.util.Date;


class Main {


  public static CharSequence createDate(long
timestamp) {

    Calendar c = Calendar.getInstance();

    c.setTimeInMillis(timestamp);

    Date d = c.getTime();

    SimpleDateFormat sdf = new
SimpleDateFormat("dd/MM/yyyy HH:mm");

    return sdf.format(d);

  }

}
```

Conclusion

Thank you again for purchasing this book!

I hope this book was able to help you get started with Android.

The next step is to study the following:

Relative, Linear, and Table Layout: When it comes to designing your app, you need to know the different types of layouts. In later versions of Android, you can use other versions of layouts, but of course, the API requirements will go up if you use them. Master these, and you will be able to design faster and cleaner.

Adding Activities or Interface: Of course, you would not want your program to contain one page only. You need more. You must let your app customers to see more content and functions. In order to do that, you will need to learn adding activities to your program. This is the part when developing your Android app will be tricky. You will not be able to rely completely on the drag and drop function and graphical layout view of Eclipse. You will need to start typing some code into your program.

Adding the Action Bar: The action bar is one of the most useful elements in Android apps. It provides the best location for the most used functions in your program. And it also aid your users when switching views, tabs, or drop down list. Chapter 7 discusses more about action bars.

Learning More about Programming: The programming course in this book is not enough to let you make 'good' programs. You should learn more about flow control statements, iteration statements, and basic creation of methods in your app. Surely, you will gain more power in creating your apps once you have a better grasp in programming in Android by writing.

Adding Event Listeners: Event listeners are there to detect if the user of your app interacted to any of the element in your app's screen. Detecting those 'events' can allow your app to react or do something in response. For example, an event that you can listen into is onClick. When your user clicks something (or clicks on a button), you can assign your program to do something like pushing a popup message on the screen.

Of course, adding event listeners will require you to program or write in your app's java file. Due to that, it is essential that you familiarize yourself with programming with Java or with the keywords and intricacies of Android apps.

Also, you should also start researching on how to import and use libraries and classes in your app. Those libraries and classes will give you access to more functions, bringing you greater freedom in your app development pursuit.

Once you have gained knowledge on those things, you will be able to launch a decent app on the market. The last thing you might want to do is to learn how to make your program support other Android devices.

You must know very well that Android devices come in all shapes and form. An Android device can be a tablet, a smartphone, or even a television. Also, they come with different screen sizes. You cannot just expect that all your customers will be using a 4-inch display smartphone. Also, you should think about the versions of Android they are using. Lastly, you must also add language options to your programs. Even though English is fine, some users will appreciate if your program caters to the primary language that they use.

And that is about it for this book. Make sure you do not stop learning Android app development.

Finally, if you enjoyed this book, please take the time to share your thoughts and post a review on Amazon. We do our best to reach out to readers and provide the best value we can. Your positive review will help us achieve that. It'd be greatly appreciated!

Thank you and good luck!

Check Out My Other Books

Below you'll find some of my other popular books that are popular on Amazon and Kindle as well. Simply click on the links below to check them out. Alternatively, you can visit my author page on Amazon to see other work done by me.

C Programming Success in a Day

Android Programming in a Day

C ++ Programming Success in a Day

Python Programming in a Day

PHP Programming Professional Made Easy

CSS Programming Professional Made Easy

Windows 8 Tips for Beginners

If the links do not work, for whatever reason, you can simply search for these titles on the Amazon website to find them.

Made in the USA
Middletown, DE
03 October 2015